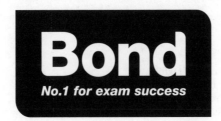

Get Ready for
Secondary School English

OXFORD
UNIVERSITY PRESS

OXFORD
UNIVERSITY PRESS

Great Clarendon Street, Oxford, OX2 6DP, United Kingdom

Oxford University Press is a department of the University of Oxford.
It furthers the University's objective of excellence in research, scholarship,
and education by publishing worldwide. Oxford is a registered trade mark of
Oxford University Press in the UK and in certain other countries

Text © Katherine Hamlyn 2015
© Oxford University Press 2015

The moral rights of the authors have been asserted

First published in 2015

British Library Cataloguing in Publication Data
Data available

978-0-19-274224-7

10 9 8 7 6 5 4 3 2 1

Printed in China

Acknowledgements

The publishers would like to thank the following for permissions to
use copyright material:

Cover illustrations: Lo Cole

Thanks to Andrew Simmons, Emma and Carrie Swann for valuable
road-testing of much of this book.

Although we have made every effort to trace and contact all
copyright holders before publication this has not been possible in all
cases. If notified, the publisher will rectify any errors or omissions at
the earliest opportunity.

Links to third party websites are provided by Oxford in good faith
and for information only. Oxford disclaims any responsibility for
the materials contained in any third party website referenced in
this work.

Contents

Introduction

About Secondary School English

This book is a step-by-step guide to learning and practising the important things you will need to know in Secondary English lessons. It can be used as a workbook because every section deals with a particular topic and has its own practice exercises. Or you can use it as a revision book and just remind yourself of the particular things you need to know. You can also use it alongside Bond Assessment Papers in English (there are six books for primary children, from age 6 to age 11) which provide sets of graded papers for development and extensive practice of English skills.

The National Strategy for Key Stage 3 has made the way English is taught in Year 7 more similar to the way it is taught in Primary schools, but there are still important differences. This book prepares you for this change and ensures you will hit the ground running when you start your new school.

How to use this book

The book is divided roughly into three sections: word level, sentence level and text level. These should be familiar to you from your work in the Literacy Hour in Primary school. Each section has a series of chapters concentrating on different aspects of English. There are practice exercises after each topic has been explained.

For every chapter, first of all read the text on the left-hand page. This tells you (or reminds you) of how to answer a certain type of question. Then practise your skills using the exercises on the right.

There are three mixed-content tests to assess how you are doing on pages 70–75. The answers are provided in a pull-out section on pages A1–A4.

The title is a brief summary of what this chapter is about.

This explains step-by-step how to tackle each sort of question on this topic.

This provides further information or important things to remember.

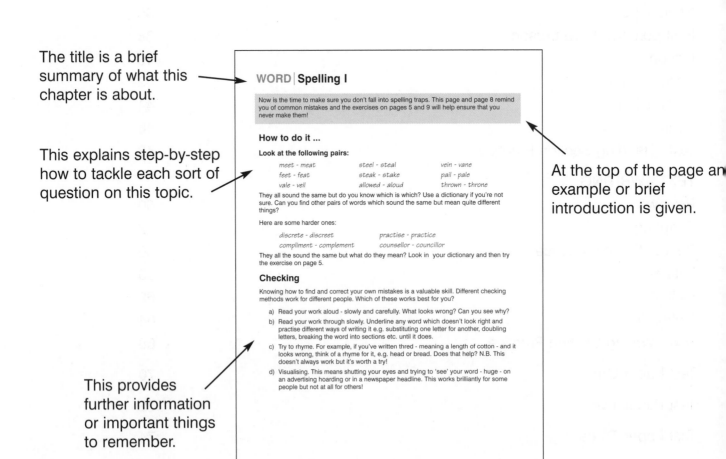

At the top of the page an example or brief introduction is given.

WORD | Spelling I

Now is the time to make sure you don't fall into spelling traps. This page and page 10 remind you of common mistakes and the exercises on pages 7 and 11 will help ensure that you never make them!

How to do it ...

Look at the following pairs:

meet – meat	*steel – steal*	*vein – vane*
feet – feat	*steak – stake*	*pail – pale*
vale – veil	*allowed – aloud*	*thrown – throne*

They all sound the same, but do you know which is which? Use a dictionary if you're not sure. Can you find other pairs of words which sound the same but mean quite different things?

Here are some harder ones:

discrete – discreet	*practise – practice*
compliment – complement	*counsellor – councillor*

They all sound the same but what do they mean? Look in your dictionary and then try the exercise on page 7.

Checking

Knowing how to find and correct your own mistakes is a valuable skill. Different checking methods work for different people. Which of these works best for you?

a) Read your work **aloud** – slowly and carefully. What looks wrong? Can you see why?

b) Read your work through **slowly**. Underline any word which doesn't look right and practise different ways of writing it, e.g. substituting one letter for another, doubling letters, breaking the word into sections etc. until it does.

c) Try to rhyme. For example, if you've written *thred* – meaning a length of cotton – and it looks wrong, think of a rhyme for it, e.g. *head* or *bread*. Does that help? This doesn't always work, but it's worth a try!

d) Visualising. This means shutting your eyes and trying to "see" your word – huge – on an advertising hoarding or in a newspaper headline. This works brilliantly for some people but not at all for others!

Finally

Here is a list of very commonly misspelled words. Learn them now!

author, completely, definite, disappear, friend, interesting, recognise, separate, sincerely, surprise, unusual

Exercises

Now practise!

---

1   Choose the correct homophone to fill each gap.

blew – blue, new – knew, witch – which, peace – piece

A storm rose. Hailstones shattered the .... of the night. The computer, ... John .... he'd turned off, flashed pink and purple. Could the .... neighbour, Mrs Chinwicket, be a ....? He'd seen her earlier, munching a .... of .... pizza. And her chimney .... orange smoke.

8

---

2   Choose the correct homophone to fill each gap.

discreet – discrete, complement – compliment,
practice – practise, counsellor – councillor

a) My mother gives advice to people who have trouble paying their bills. She is called a debt ....

b) I am playing in a concert on Saturday and have to .... hard every night this week.

c) Waders and divers are two .... groups within the whole range of water birds.

d) Tell Neelam and Jack about the party but be ....! It's a surprise for Nick and he knows nothing about it!

e) Ketchup is the perfect .... to fish and chips, I think, though some people prefer tartare sauce.

f) I go to football .... on Saturday mornings and come home covered in mud.

g) We're trying to get a Controlled Parking Scheme in our area and we're writing to our local .... to ask her to help.

h) I don't mind how much you tell me I look wonderful. You can't .... me too often!

8

---

3   Correct this passage using one or more of the methods on page 6.

Dan and Deepak started a buisness making biskits. They tried several recipies, which were all delishus. "We have to discide which one," said Deepak. Dan ran his tounge round his lips. "I need to try them again," he said, "it's probaly the raisin crunch but the butterscotch was espeshully good too." Finaly they picked their favoret. "Lemon crisp it is!" cried Deepak exitedly – but Dan had disappered to be sick.

12

28
TOTAL

WORD | Vocabulary I

Surnames – research time!

English surnames come from various sources. The first *Mr Williamson*, for instance, would, of course, have been the son of someone called *William*. *Peterson*, *Thomson*, *Dickson* and many others were derived in the same way. Ancestors of people with the surnames *Bolton*, *Warwick*, *Durham*, and so on would probably have come from those places. Many people have surnames that derive from the jobs their ancestors did. *Baker* and *Miller* are obvious examples, as are *Teacher*, *Thatcher* and *Potter*.

How to do it ...

But what did the ancestors of people called *Fletcher*, *Smith*, *Farrier*, *Cooper*, *Palmer*, *Barker*, *Napier*, *Spencer*, *Fuller* or *Turner* do? Use your dictionary or other reference books, or maybe the Internet, to find out!

Then see what you can discover about people called *Wright* or people whose names end in *wright* such as *Arkwright*, *Wainwright*, *Plowright*, *Cartwright* – and others. Does this tell you anything about the world our forefathers lived in when surnames began to be fixed, in about the twelfth century?

Other languages and cultures are just as interesting when it comes to surnames. Sometimes, as with English, their surnames come from parents, places or jobs. In Germany, for instance, *Schneider* is a common name – *schneider* is German for *tailor* (*Taylor*!). In France, *Boucher* is common – *boucher* is French for *butcher*. In Chinese the common name *Wong* means a field or wide stretch of water, and *Chan* means old. In the Sikh religion, all women have *Kaur*, which means *princess*, as a surname and all men have *Singh*, which means *lion*, as a surname or middle name.

Why do the Irish have an *O'* in front of many of their surnames? And why do the Scots have *Mac*? Why do the Germans often have *von* in between the first names and surnames, and the Dutch have *van*? Many Arabic names have *bin* or *ibn* in the same place, and modern Hebrew has *ben*. Many Armenian names end in *ian* or *ion*, Polish names end in *ski* or *ska*, and Russian names often end in *ov* or *ova* (why the differences?). Russian names also often end in *vitch* – can you find out why? These questions can provide an interesting research project and good practice for senior school!

If you don't already know it, try to discover the origin of your own surname and those of members of your wider family, friends and neighbours. You will be very surprised to find out what some names mean!

Finally, have you noticed how often people seem to have the right (wrong?) surname for their job? For example, the dentist called Mr Fang, the undertaker called Doug Graves, the plumbers called Dampier and Whetham, the physiotherapist called Mrs Paine.

Have fun matching up your own list of jobs to the names of the people who do them.

Exercises

Now practise!

Now let's try something different – adverbs

These are useful words which tell you more about **how**, **when** or **where** a verb (doing word) is done. They can make your writing more interesting and give it more character. Adverbs are words like *hurriedly*, *sleepily*, *fast*, *late*, *angrily*, *here*, *carefully*.

1 See how much livelier you can make this story by putting adverbs in the spaces.

Mum worked .... over that salmon. It was huge and she cooked it .... , having washed it .... and .... surrounded it in the fish kettle with lots of herbs and vegetables. When it was ready, she removed it .... and placed it on a special dish. Then she rested it .... on a chair while she laid the table. She left the room .... to fetch some forks and was surprised to see Ruggles slinking .... out of the room on her return. She could hardly believe her eyes. There, on the dish, was a .... cleaned salmon skeleton.

9

Adverbs of time

All 9 adverbs below have a sense of **time**. Put them in order of frequency with *never* at one end and *always* at the other. NB Many are interchangeable.

rarely, frequently, always, often, occasionally, never, infrequently, usually, sometimes

2 Now fill in the gaps below using whichever adverb of time you think best.

    a) No matter what the time of year, the sun .... rises each morning.

    b) Despite snowy pictures on cards, we .... have a white Christmas.

    c) In Great Britain, we normally have General Elections every five years, but .... the interval is shorter.

    d) As I make it a priority, I .... manage to see my team's home matches.

    e) John and Dan run equally fast; .... John wins and other times Dan does.

    f) I mean to remember my keys but somehow I .... leave them at home.

    g) You must know that I would .... do anything to hurt you.

    h) I wish you wouldn't forget to give me my phone messages so ....

    i) I love looking at stars, but the city is so lit-up that only .... can I see them.

3 Now use each of the 9 adverbs of time above in a sentence of your own.

18

27
TOTAL

WORD | Spelling II

Prefixes and suffixes

You'll remember that these are groups of letters which go at the beginning or the end of words to change them into other words. Occasionally they can cause havoc with spelling! Make sure you're clear about *dis...* and *...ly*.

How to do it ...

dis...

It goes at the beginning of many words, usually changing them into their own opposites, e.g. *agree → disagree, inherit → disinherit, trust → distrust*. It doesn't alter the spelling of the original word. For example, *appear* becomes **dis***appear* (no additional "s", no dropping of a "p"), *satisfied* becomes **dis***satisfied* (no dropping of an "s"). Look at other *dis-* words in your dictionary. You'll be amazed at how many there are! Notice, though, that not all of them are opposites, e.g. *dispute, distort, disdain*.

...ly

It goes at the end of adjectives (words that describe nouns) to change them into adverbs (words that tell you more about verbs), e.g. *silent* (a silent dog) → *silently* (the dog stared silently). *ly* only changes the spelling of the word it comes after when:

a) the word ends in *...y*, e.g. *happy → happily, necessary → necessarily, noisy → noisily* or

b) the word ends in two vowels, e.g. *due → duly, true → truly* or

c) there are two consonants before a final "e", e.g. *simple → simply, nimble → nimbly*.

Otherwise the word stays the same, e.g. *normal → normally, helpful → helpfully* (no dropping of an "l"), *wise → wisely, sane → sanely* (no dropping of an "e").

NB Whatever the word, *ly* is **always** *ly* – never *ley*!

Doubled letters

Whether you have one "p" or two "p"s in a word can make all the difference. For example, look at this sentence:

*Yasmin's ankle hurt so much she had to go **hoping** all the way home.*

Or this one:

*Yasmin tore the paper off her presents **hopping** to find the roller blades she wanted.*

Do you get the point? This is important when words end in *...ing* or *...ed*.

A trick to remember here is that when the vowel in a word is **long**, i.e. it sounds like its name, as in *tape, dine, hope* or *resume*, the final consonant is **never** doubled when *...ing* or *...ed* come after it. If the vowel is **short**, as in *tap, win, hop* or *strum*, the final consonant is **always** doubled when *...ing* or *...ed* comes after it, e.g. *tapping, winning, hopping, strumming*. The most commonly doubled letters are *b, l, m, n, p* and *t*. Now find examples of your own.

Exercises

Now practise!

1 Add *dis…* to the beginning of the following words and use each new word to write a sentence of your own.

appointed, allowed, able, believe, connect, honest, loyal, service, obey, similar

mis… works in much the same way and does much the same job as *dis…* . Look up the following words in your dictionary and use each one in a sentence of your own:

misalliance, misbehave, miscue, misfire, misinform, mismatch, misshapen, misspell, mistake, mistrust

2 Change the following adjectives into adverbs by adding …*ly*.

true, wise, sleepy, nice, wonderful, humble, actual, healthy, usual, cheery

Now use each adverb in a sentence of your own.

30

3 Doubled letters

Complete the words in the following passage by adding …*ing* or …*ed*. Remember to double the last consonant letter where necessary.

Neelam was sit........... in the vet's waiting room pat........... her dog. Her mother had stop........... her from bunking off school to look after Ruggles ever since he'd stun........... himself div........... into the lake on Sunday. Neelam had gone wad........... in to save him and had arrived home drip........... wet, holding a very dazed dog. She blam........... herself for the accident and felt terrible. She had rub........... Ruggles down before get........... into her own bath. When they were both dry, she had drag........... him onto her bed and they had both drop........... off. Now, whil........... away the time by gaz........... into Ruggles' eyes, Neelam just wished it had never happened.

4 Now write one sentence for each of the following words:

robed, robbed; taped, tapped; filed, filled; slimed, slimmed; fused, fussed

You can see it matters which you choose!

If you're still unsure about single and double letters, think about "the man who felt furry when his wife ate the entire desert."

24

54
TOTAL

11

WORD | Vocabulary II

How to do it ...

Read the following passage:

"No sleepover," **said** *Deepak's Mum. "Last time there were crisps all over the floor and I found my best vase in the freezer."*

"But Mum!" **said** *Deepak, "everyone else has sleepovers."*

"If everyone else jumped off Blackpool tower would you want to too?" **said** *his Mum, as he knew she would.*

"But it's not fair," *he* **said**, *"it's my turn!"*

"Have a nice tea party with John and Neelam," *she* **said**.

"A nice tea party!" **said** *Deepak. "Oh why didn't I get Dan's Mum,"* *he* **said**, *"instead of the most uncool Mum in Britain?"*

Now read it again, substituting the *said*s with the following words:

insisted, pleaded, inquired, wailed, suggested, exploded, sighed

You can see that the piece is suddenly much livelier.

Write your own conversation using *said* not more than once. If you need reminding about the punctuation and layout of conversation, look at page 30. You may like to choose one of the following titles:

> *Heard Outside the Staffroom Door*
>
> *The Day I Brought Home My New Pet*
>
> *Explaining to Mr Snapperchild Why I Hadn't Got My Homework*
>
> *A Row with My Best Friend*
>
> *A Mealtime at Home*

Exercises

Now practise!

Now let's try something different – prepositions

Prepositions are usually short words that give a sense of direction or place. Some common prepositions are:

up, down, in, out, into, onto, at, to, from, for, with, without, under, over, above, below, through, around, about, along, between, beneath, of, before, after

It can sometimes be quite difficult to know which preposition to use.

1   Fill the gaps in the following passage with the most appropriate prepositions from the list above:

Dan wriggled .... the fence, getting his chest covered .... mud and tearing holes .... his fleece. "I'm done ....," he thought and, keeping his head ...., pulled himself .... his feet and started to dodge .... the trees. He listened .... for the sounds of the hunters and their dogs but he could hear nothing .... the noise of the wind rushing .... his hair. "Just let me get .... the open," he thought. "I could skirt .... the farm and .... the canal if I can just get out .... the woods .... they catch ....
me."

We often attach prepositions to verbs in a way which has little or nothing to do with their usual meaning. Imagine how confusing some of the following expressions might be to a person learning English as a foreign language:

to put up with someone, to put someone up, to be put out, to put your back out, to put your back into something, the output of a company, to put out a fire or a light, to put someone down, to put an animal down, to put your name down, to put someone off, to be put off something, to put one over on someone

17

17
TOTAL

WORD | Vocabulary II

How to do it ...

Try a similar exercise with *went*. In the following passage substitute the *went*s with more interesting verbs of your own.

*Yasmin had wanted to go to Megaland as long as she could remember. Once through the gates she **went** on everything. She **went** down the "Gyrating-Giraffe" three times, **went** over the terrifying "Death Drop" twice, **went** round the "Zoomer" so fast that she couldn't stand up afterwards, **went** up the "Hellter-Skullter" in total darkness and **went** out again, screaming but loving it, **went** along the "Snake Ladder" not daring to look down and **went** home again asking when she could go back.*

Now write your own piece about an active day, trying not to use *went* more than once. You may like to choose one of the following titles.

A Trip to the Sea/a Theme Park/Disneyland/the Fair/the Sports Centre, Sports Day, Climbing a Mountain, Going Shopping, A Camping Holiday

Hint: It's quite surprising how many words for *speaking* and *going* we borrow from those we associate with animals.

For example: *John **roared** at the goalie, Deepak **hissed** to his sister, Mr Snapperchild **snarled** at 4b, Yasmin **hooted** with laughter or Mrs Chinwicket **scampered** up the stairs, Neelam **crawled** into bed, John's little sister **trotted** after her dad, Dan **flew** down the road.*

You can have fun making a collection of these and using them in your own writing. You could probably find up to 200 substitutes for *said* if you involve friends and family and maybe 100 or so for *went*.

Exercises

Now practise!

Here are some more commonly-used preposition/verb combinations made with the everyday verbs: *do, make, take, break* and *give*:

to do *someone in, to do someone over, to do a house up, to do someone out of something, to do without something, to do someone down, to do for someone*

to make *up with someone, to make someone up, to make something up, to make do with something, to make out, to make from somewhere, to make to somewhere*

to take *someone in, to take someone out, to take someone down a peg, to take something up, to take someone up, to take out or take away, to take over a business*

to break *off, to break up, to break out, to break in, to break down, to break away*

to give *up, to give out, to give over, to give away, to give in, to give way*

1   Make sure you know what all these expressions mean. Look them up in a good dictionary if necessary. Then make up a story of your own, using as many of these as you can.

2   See if you can recall or find out combinations which are made with prepositions and the following verbs: *fit, set, call, get, hold, pay.*

Finally, can you live up to your parents' expectations while you try to live down your behaviour last Sunday when you were living it up? Can you live with the memory?

11

WORD | Dictionary work I

Your dictionary is your best friend when it comes to anything involving words. In addition to being the most useful book for English work, it is a source of information on history, geography, science, other languages – everything. This unit will help you to explore your own dictionary and discover its riches.

How to do it ...

Get hold of as large a dictionary as possible, as a small one doesn't have room for all the fascinating information you'll want. Try to invest in one that's too big for even a very big pocket! See if you can find one or two dictionaries of foreign languages too, for some of these exercises. Begin by looking at the page – usually at the front – that explains abbreviations used in the entries. You'll need to get to know these.

1 Let's start with the subjects on your school timetable. Why is *geography* called *geography*? Look up these words to see where they come from: *geography, history, science, physics, chemistry, biology, information technology, design* – any others? *Science* is an interesting one, isn't it? Does it make you want to learn Latin?

2 Many words come from Latin (*L* in your dictionary), brought here by the Romans over 2000 years ago. Many come from French (*F* or *Fr*), brought here by William the Conqueror nearly 1000 years ago. Others are Old English (*O E*) or Anglo-Saxon (*AS*). Some were brought by the Vikings – we call their language Old Norse (*O N*). More recently, words have come into our language from everywhere in the world as a result of travel, colonisation, the mass media and so on.

Plunder your dictionary to see where these words came from:

sofa, banana, chicken, flapjack, mob, verandah, sleep, television, chortle, bumf (this one is rude!)

Where do our days of the week come from? And our months of the year?

3 What did the following originally mean?

salary, khaki, spinster, cavalier, gentle, gossip, husband, natural, nice

4 Use your dictionary to explain the connection between the following words in each group:
a) *meter, metre, mete, metric, symmetry*
b) *symmetry, synonym, similar, simultaneous*
c) *synonym, anonymous, pseudonym, acronym, antonym*
d) *combine, collect, conspire, connect*
e) *independent, pendulum, pendant, depends*

5 Numbers. Try to find out what the numbers one to ten are in other languages. Make a table with a column for each language you investigate. You'll find some surprising things!

6 Try to find out what the following words are in other languages (Welsh is a good one for these!):

blue, school, flat, cold, fire, church, table, board

Exercises

Now practise!

We tend to think of the words in each of these two groups of words as having similar meanings. Can you find their original meanings?

1 a) *fantastic*   b) *awful*
         fabulous   *frightful*
         wonderful   *horrible*
         marvellous   *dreadful*
         terrific   *ghastly*

2   Look up the derivations of the following words and write down an explanation of each one: *goodbye, nickname, chum, fortnight, naughty, alphabet, pantomime*

3   Where in the world did the following words come from?

chocolate, pyjamas, toboggan, berserk, tycoon, ghoul, hurricane, robot

4   Find out how the following everyday things get their names:

Wellingtons, Braille, sandwiches, cardigan, teddy bears, cheddar, jersey, biro, Hoover, pasteurised milk

35

5   Lewis Carroll – as you may well have discovered on page 16 – liked making up new and expressive words. In *Jabberwocky* he made up *galumph* from *gallop* and *triumph*, *slithy* from *lithe* and *slimy* and *mimsy* from *flimsy* and *miserable* – in addition to the one we met earlier! You can have great fun making up your own. How about *weeble* – from *weak* and *feeble*? Or *stunchy* from *crunchy* and *sticky*? Try and make up 10 words of your own and then see if you can work them into a story or poem of your own or, if you like, a recipe! How about a recipe for *Stunchy Buffins*?

6   Finally, lexicography (the making of dictionaries) is not easy work. How would you define the meaning of the following words to someone who had never heard them before?

table, light, soft, fork, today, water, dog, think, box, sweet

NB If in doubt, check it out! John was once given a title with the word MOLESTATION in it. He wrote in a lively way about a place where trains stopped to let on and off small black furry creatures who make hills. Perhaps he should have looked it up ...!

"Lexicographer": A writer of dictionaries, a harmless drudge.

Dr Samuel Johnson's definition in his own dictionary

20

55
TOTAL

WORD | Apostrophes

These little punctuation marks need to be in the right place and **only** in the right place. Perhaps you need to remind yourself about where they go and where they **don't** go!

How to do it ...

Apostrophes **don't** go in straightforward plurals, e.g. *dogs, shops, creatures, girls, parents, tomatoes, chips, disc jockeys, footballers, peas.*

They **do** go in two very precise places:

1 Apostrophes show that **one or more letters have been missed out**. They go exactly (not somewhere nearby!) where the missed letters would have been:

   have not → haven't, should have → should've, I will → I'll, Neelam is coming → Neelam's coming, Yasmin will laugh → Yasmin'll laugh

2 Apostrophes of possession show that **something belongs to someone**. They go after the last letter of the person or people to which the thing belongs:

   John's dog, Neelam's house, Mrs Chinwicket's garden, the teacher's car, Mr Harris's fork, the women's room

The *s* normally added after the apostrophe is omitted if the thing is owned by more than one person, e.g. *the teachers' meeting, the ladies' cloakroom.* This is to do with the way it sounds. In all other cases, the *s* to show belonging comes after the apostrophe which goes after the last letter of whoever owns the thing, e.g. *Thomas's dog, John's shoes, Neelam's mum, Mrs Das's house, the innkeeper's pub.*

Practice

1 Shorten the following into their usual abbreviated forms, e.g. *I have → I've:*

   is not, you are, she is, they will, Mrs Chinwicket is, we had, can not, should have, do not, we are, would have, are not, you have, he will, could have, were not, would not, I am, they are, she has, I had

2 Write the following, using apostrophes of possession as in the example given.

the fur of the dog	*the dog's fur*
the ears of the rabbit	-----------------------
the team of the men	-----------------------
the webs of the spiders	-----------------------
the boots of the boy	-----------------------
the hats of the model	-----------------------
the book of Thomas	-----------------------
the work of the artists	-----------------------
the hive of the bees	-----------------------
the pictures of the boys	-----------------------
the party of the children	-----------------------
the home of the ladies	-----------------------
the clothes of the girl	-----------------------

Now check Exercise 2 **carefully**. Have you, in each case, put the apostrophe after the **last letter** of whoever the thing belongs to? **Are you sure**?

33

Exercises

Now practise!

3   Add the missing apostrophes in the following passage. Concentrate hard and remember the rules. There are 24 of both kinds to put in.

NB *Its* and *it's*. *It's* is the short form of *it is* or *it has*. *Its* means **belonging to it**, e.g. the door has lost *its* handle. In this way *its* is like *his* – you'd never put an apostrophe in *his*, now would you?

Whats the new boys name, I wonder? Hes looking as though hes lost his way and his backpacks splitting its sides with all the new books. Hes sitting on Deepaks table but hes in Yasmins group for Maths and Johns for English. Ive got him for Mr Snapperchilds lesson and hell need warning about that. Hes left his coat in the boys cloakroom but his trainers are in the teachers lockers and they wont like that. He looks as if hed be quite fun so Ill see if hell sit next to me for Ms Mosss class and maybe itll be less boring than usual. Then its the Snapperchild and youre never really prepared for that! I wonder whose bus he goes home on?

24

4   Read the following passage and underline the correct alternative in the brackets:

(Dan's/Dans) lost his cat. (Dan's/Dans) (cat's/cats) name is Goblin. (Its/It's) jet black and has blue eyes and (it's/its) never been any good at finding (it's/its) way home. Dan put up a notice in Mrs (Dass/Das's) window but (no-ones/no-one's) rung up so far. Goblin disappeared once before and the caretaker found him in the (boys'/boy's) cloakroom at the sports pitch. I don't think (cats'/cat's) memories can be very good, or maybe they just like a change now and then.

5   Now write one sentence for each of the following phrases:
   a) Deepak's trainers
   b) couldn't help it
   c) the cats' holiday home
   d) the bus's tyre
   e) the farmers' market
   f) Dan's knees
   g) my school's hall
   h) its mother
   i) the books' covers
   j) Mr Snapperchild'll

20

77
TOTAL

WORD | Section practice

Ijah's First Day

That's the boy who showed me around. His name is Deepak. After the secretary showed me into the classroom, he came in and then three of his friends showed up. They're all in my class – that's 4b.

In France, where I was before, school started very early. I prefer it here. It's funny having to wear **uniform** here. We could wear **denims** or **jeans** of any kind there – whatever we liked. We called the teachers by their first names and could go in and out of the staffroom.

It's not like that here. The teachers' room is out of bounds and they've a seperate dining room too. I'm not in favour of that. Perhaps they get better food than us!

Mr Thresher is nice and Miss Harridan's class seems happy, but Mr Snapperchild is a nightmare! I expect he's got a home of his own but it's easy to believe he just sinks back into the furniture at night and haunts the school like a **ghoul**.

Those children are in a **queue**, patiently waiting for **vaccinations**. My turn tomorrow. That teacher's going to the art room to use the **guillotine**. There's Deepak again. He's got a really cool **mobile** and his dad drives a Ferrari. I think he shows off a bit. His friend's arm's in plaster. Perhaps I'll get to write on it.

Read the passage carefully and find the following.

a) Two adverbs of time, two adverbs of place (telling you where something is done).

b) A verb which is used four times, each time with a different preposition, each time making a phrase with a totally different meaning.

c) Apostrophes showing missed letters and showing belonging. How many of each are there?

d) An adverb which has been made by adding ...*ly* to an adjective.

e) One word that has been deliberately misspelled.

f) Use your dictionary to find out about the origins of the words in bold type.

g) Thresher and Harridan sound acceptable names for teachers. Might this always have been so?

h) Apart from the prepositions you found for question (b), how many others are there?

i) Write the conversation Deepak has with his friends about the new boy, Ijah. He will want to report to them about his conversation with Ijah when they went round the school together. Check over your work carefully using whatever methods work best for you. Pay special attention to your use of apostrophes and the correct punctuation of conversation. (See pages 18, 19 and 30 if you need reminding.)

55

55
TOTAL

SENTENCE | Phrases

Prepositional phrases

Phrases are little groups of words. There are various kinds of phrases. *Prepositional phrases* begin with prepositions, as you saw on page 13. They include:

of, in, up, at, with, to, from, for, under, over, out, through, around, after, onto, between, about, during

How to do it ...

Phrases don't have verbs in them but they are useful in different ways. Sometimes we use them to give more information. For example:

> The noise *of the traffic* kept me awake.
> The man *in the next seat* is snoring.
> The walk *to school* gets longer each day.

All these phrases begin with a preposition and none of them includes a verb. Look at how, if you take the phrases away, the sentences still make sense but give less information. This is not always the case. "The baby kept them *up all night*" doesn't really mean anything without the prepositional phrase.

You can use phrases to make your writing more interesting. In the following passage, the prepositional phrases in *italics* are not strictly necessary to the story but it would be duller without them! The preposition at the start of each phrase is in **bold**.

The man **in** *the ancient raincoat* and the dog **with** *the crooked tail* pushed on **down** *the puddled road* **into** *the howling wind.* **In** *the dim lamplight* the man stared **through** *the shop window* and his eyes watered **in** *the harsh wind.* **Under** *a propped-up dustbin lid*, the dog spotted a cat crunching a fish-head **with** *great enjoyment.* **After** *a moment's thought*, the cat decided to ignore the dog **with** *the scruffy tail* but while the man was staring **at** *all the beautiful things in the shop*, the dog swore **by** *The Great Bone* that, when they next met, it would mean a fight **to** *the death!*

If you read through the story without the prepositional phrases, there's not much of it left, is there? It's worthwhile remembering this if you're the sort of person who needs reminding to put more description in your stories. This is one way to do it!

You may now like to take the basic story (the bits not in *italics*) and substitute phrases of your own. You can make it into a rather different story!

"Good phrases are surely, and ever were, very commendable."

Shakespeare

Exercises

Now practise!

1   Underline all the prepositional phrases in the following sentences and ring the preposition with which they start. For example: *Our garden, ⟨during⟩ the winter, gets covered ⟨with⟩ leaves.* NB There may be more than one phrase in a sentence!

a) All the boys in my class are mad about football.

b) Television before tea switches my brain off.

c) Mrs Chinwicket's neighbours in Grimley Road are used to interesting events of all kinds.

d) The Head Teacher of Grimley Junior School is a very kind man.

e) *The Hound of the Baskervilles* is a famous story by Sir Arthur Conan Doyle.

f) The classroom behind the hall was sending out strange noises into the corridor.

g) I like crumpets with maple syrup for tea.

Read through the sentences again, leaving out the prepositional phrases. All the sentences still make sense, don't they?

12

2   Make the following sentences more interesting by adding prepositional phrases. Remember, these phrases must start with a preposition and do not have a verb. You can use the prepositions in Exercise 1 but think of some of your own too.

a) The house .... needs a new roof.

b) The man .... is fixing an oil leak.

c) Mr Snapperchild's lesson .... is the one everyone tries to get out of.

d) Children .... can audition for the play.

e) Latecomers .... will not be admitted.

f) Rain .... has ruined the game.

g) The supermarket .... has my favourite chocolate biscuits ....

3   Now make up sentences of your own including the following prepositional phrases:

around the corner, in my room, after school, under the stairs, during lunchbreak, through the bushes, between my teeth, onto the floor, from Auntie Marianne, at Granny's flat

4   We use common prepositional phrases all the time such as: *up in arms, at sixes and sevens, on tenterhooks, out of luck, from pillar to post.* See how many more of these you can find.

5   Write a short story or description of your own in which you include at least three prepositional phrases. You may like to call it: *Making Dinner* or *Mrs Chinwicket's Birthday*.

20

32
TOTAL

SENTENCE | Clauses I

Main clauses and adjectival clauses

Clauses are groups of words that must include a subject (the person(s) or thing(s) that the clause is about) and a verb (a doing word). So, *the three boys chatted* is a clause, *the three boys* being the subject and *chatted* being the verb.

How to do it ...

All sentences must have at least one clause – a *main* clause. A main clause may have as few as two words in it, so long as one is a noun and acts as the subject of the sentence and the other is a verb, e.g. *Dan shouted, Neelam kicked, Mr Snapperchild snarled, Yasmin slept.*

Many sentences have two or more clauses. These usually consist of a main clause and subordinate clauses. A subordinate clause is one that depends for its meaning on the main clause and would make no sense on its own. (They are sometimes called **dependent** clauses.)

The dog rushed around the park *which is near my house.*

In the above sentence, the part in bold is the main clause. It makes sense on its own. The part in italics makes no sense on its own but it tells you more about the park. It is a *subordinate adjectival clause* – adjectival because, like an adjective, it tells you more about a noun – in this case, *the park*. (You may sometimes see adjectival clauses called **relative** clauses.) The verb in this clause is *is*.

Here are some more examples:

a) **My mum likes the <u>woman</u>** *who runs the antique shop on Grimley Broadway.*
b) **Deepak's dad owns a <u>racehorse</u>** *that ran in The Grand National.*

You can see how the subordinate adjectival clause tells you more about a noun in the main clause, in this case, a) woman and b) racehorse.

Sometimes these subordinate clauses are embedded in the main clause. In the sentence below the part in **bold** is the main clause. It could stand on its own. The part in *italics*, telling you more about the dog, is the subordinate adjectival clause and could not stand on its own.

The dog *which belongs to my friend* **hates walks in the rain.**

These clauses usually begin with *who* or *which* (though *that, when* and *where* are also common). Here are some more examples. See how sometimes the subordinate clause (in *italics*) is inside the main clause (in **bold**). Which word begins each subordinate clause?

a) **The girl** *who brought in the guinea pig* **came from Trembly Juniors.**
b) **Deepak's house,** *where the meeting is happening,* **is in Grimley Crescent.**
c) **The car** *that I bought yesterday* **has a scratch.**
d) **Miss Harridan bought a paper** *which advertises jobs.*
e) **The time** *when the train should arrive* **hasn't been announced yet.**

Exercises

Now practise!

1 Underline the **main** clause in the following sentences. Remember that the subordinate adjectival clause may be embedded in it. Take care to underline all the words that belong to the main clause. It helps to start by underlining the verbs – one per clause.

a) I like stations that have lots of shops in them.

b) Trains that cross continental Europe sometimes go through very long tunnels.

c) The guard who took our passports was very knowledgeable about the area.

d) The day that I get to India will be the best day of my life.

e) Hotel managers are quite used to tourists who arrive late.

f) The café where I left my wallet was very crowded.

6

2 Sentences can have more than one main clause. Two main clauses can be joined by *and*, *but* and *or*. Sentences can also have more than one subordinate clause. How many clauses of each kind are there in the following sentences? Underline the main clauses and ring the subordinate adjectival ones. **Remember that a clause must have a verb in it!**

a) John ate his beans, which were cold, and he dropped the plate, which broke.

b) Deepak, who loves pizzas with different toppings, makes his own at home.

c) Mr Snapperchild was not pleased with the girls who had filled his wellies with sand.

d) Dan could go to Russia or he might fly to Venezuela, where he has relations.

e) Ijah raced round the corner and he charged up the road, which was very icy, and he leapfrogged the railings and he slid into the duckpond.

f) My auntie, who loves animals, has six cats, four canaries, an Alsatian, a rabbit and seven gerbils.

6

3 The following passage has main clauses and gaps where subordinate adjectival clauses could go. The leading word, e.g. *who* or *which*, of the subordinate clause is given to you. Make up your own clauses to fill in the gaps.

Grimley Park, which _____, has brilliant football pitches next to the prison. Rob the trainer, who _____, meets us there on Saturday mornings. All the boys who _____ practise for an hour and a half till twelve. The boys who _____ get chosen for the team which_____. Away games, which _____, can take all afternoon. Some clubs which _____ give you tea afterwards but my mum, who _____, gets cross if I'm not hungry for my dinner. John and Dan, who _____, also come along but no-one is as good as Ijah, who _____.

10

22 TOTAL

25

SENTENCE | Clauses II

Subordinate adverbial clauses

Look back at pages 24 and 25 and the work on subordinate adjectival clauses. Adjectival clauses tell you more about the noun or nouns in the main clause. Another kind of subordinate – or dependent – clause, is the **adverbial** clause, which tells you more about the verb in the main clause. Subordinate adverbial clauses do the same job as simple adverbs but are groups of words that include a verb.

How to do it ...

Here are some examples. The main clause is in **bold** and the subordinate adverbial clause is in *italics*:

  a) **I ate my dinner** *as fast as I could*. (The subordinate adverbial clause tells you more about **ate**, i.e. **how I ate**.)
  b) **We rowed across the lake** *when the moon was high in the sky*. (The subordinate adverbial clause tells you **when** we **rowed**.)
  c) **The new school was built** *where the old hospital had been*. (The subordinate adverbial clause tells you more about **built**, i.e. **where** it was built.)
  d) **Neelam dived into the river** *so that she might save the cat*. (The adverbial clause tells you the **purpose** of **dived**.)
  e) **Yasmin worked so hard on her project** *that her teacher gave her a gold star*. (The adverbial clause tells you the **result** of **worked**.)
  f) *Although he had only just arrived,* **Ijah was made captain**. (The adverbial clause makes a **concession**, i.e. it explains why there are **special circumstances** about **was made**.)
  g) **Mr Snapperchild shouted for twenty minutes** *because everyone had forgotten their trainers*. (The adverbial clause gives the **reason** for **shouted**.)
  h) *If it snows* **we can have PE outside**. (The adverbial clause tells you the **condition** on which **can have** depends.)

Sometimes a sentence starts with a main clause. Sometimes it can start with a subordinate clause. You can find examples of both in the sentences above. It makes no difference. The clue to finding clauses is always to start by finding **finite verbs**. A finite verb is not an infinitive, e.g. *to eat, to work, to sleep,* nor a participle on its own, e.g. *walking, celebrating, slipping*. It is a **doing word** which, together with a subject, makes a complete clause that makes sense, e.g. *Dan **thought**, Yasmin **threw**, Mrs Chinwicket **stirs**.* As in some of the examples above, finite verbs can be in two or three parts, e.g. *Deepak's dad **will travel**, I **have begun**, we **will be going**.* If you find a finite verb – you have a clause!

There are 10 clauses in this short passage. Can you spot them all?

Dan's uncle has an Italian restaurant and Dan eats there most Sundays. He took Neelam there last Sunday. They ate masses of pasta and delicious ice cream. If she asked for it, she could have wine, Dan said! Neelam thought Dan was quite different in the restaurant because he spoke Italian all the time!

Exercises

Now practise!

1 Underline the finite verbs in this passage. Remember that sometimes finite verbs can be in two or even three parts.

John and Yasmin are making flapjacks. They have poured some oats into a bowl and are melting butter and sugar together. Yesterday they made coconut biscuits but John's dad ate them all while he watched snooker on the TV. John is greasing the baking tin while Yasmin mixes the oats with the melted butter. Although Yasmin adores flapjacks, she says she won't eat any because she plans to take them into school for Neelam's birthday. John licks the spoon while Neelam is wiping the worktop and Neelam licks the bowl while John fills the dishwasher.

2 Read the following passage carefully. Underline all the finite verbs. Then try to find all the main clauses and underline them in a different colour. Finally, ring all the subordinate adverbial clauses. In each case, work out what information they are giving you about the verb in the main clause.

Ijah is very good at tree houses. He went into the woods the day after school had broken up. Deepak and John went too so that Ijah could teach them about tree house techniques. Because it was winter, their hands got very cold and they had to wear gloves. John worked as hard as he could. He carried branches until his back ached. Ijah stacked them up where they were out of the wind. Although the boys worked hard all day, the tree house was still only a pile of branches by sunset. After they had worked for three whole days, they held a tree house-warming party.

52

3 Write your own sentences, each one with a main clause and a subordinate adverbial clause. Start each sentence with the main clause. The subordinate clauses should start with one of the following words or phrases. Use each one once.

where, until, why, as, because, since, although, how, so that, when

4 Now write 10 more sentences, this time starting each one with a subordinate adverbial clause. Start each sentence with one of the words from the list in Exercise 3.

5 Think about the order of clauses. For example, does the sentence have a different emphasis if you put the main clause first? Consider the following examples and then think up some of your own.

a) *Although I don't like her much, I shared my sweets with Yasmin. / I shared my sweets with Yasmin, although I don't like her much.*

b) *The firemen arrived when the fire was nearly out. / When the fire was nearly out, the firemen arrived.*

20

72
TOTAL

SENTENCE | Organising sentences

As we have seen in our pages on clauses, although we can read and write sentences without thinking too much about it, they are actually quite complicated things to organise! How clever we are to be able to manage so well! It's a bit like using buildings with lots of rooms and doors and floors and lifts. We go in and out and up and down with no problem and don't think about how complicated it really is! Sometimes it helps to think for a moment about some of the ways in which we organise our sentences so cleverly.

How to do it ...

One useful tool we have to help us organise sentences is *connective* words. There are various kinds of connectives. Some are usually found at the start of sentences. Others join two clauses in a sentence; these are called *conjunctions*. There are two kinds. The most common conjunctions are *and*, *but* and *or*. These words join together two clauses of equal importance, such as two main clauses, as in the following examples:

a) *Ijah is good at running,* **and** *he can speak perfect French.*

b) *I am intending to go to India,* **but** *I might change my mind.*

c) *Neelam will meet me at the cinema,* **or** *she will pick me up at home.*

Think of a see-saw – the middle bit doesn't move but holds the centre between the two equal sides. That's how these **coordinating conjunctions** work.

The second kind of connectives are **subordinating conjunctions**. These link main clauses to subordinate clauses. Examples of subordinating conjunctions are: *when, while, before, after, until, if, because, although, that, since*

See how they are used in the following sentences. Remember that the main clause need not come first:

a) I was late *because* the bus didn't come.

b) *Although* Mr Snapperchild never smiled, Deepak once heard him snigger.

c) Yasmin waited *while* Neelam laced her trainers.

Connectives like these conjunctions help to make a piece of writing flow. Look at the following passage. The conjunctions are in brackets. Read the passage aloud without saying the conjunctions. Then read it again with the conjunctions. Can you see how much better it is as a piece of writing with the conjunctions?

John hated walks (until) he got the dog. Deepak swears he never went out (before) the dog came. Now John's in the park all day waiting (while) the dog chases squirrels. Deepak wants a dog too (although) he knows his dad won't let him have one. Ijah's training hard (because) he wants to beat John's dog in a race.

> *"Never a word fills a bonnier function*
> *Than a well-placed conjunction!"*
>
> Anon

Exercises

Now practise!

1 Choose the best conjunction from the list to fill in the gaps. You don't need to use all the conjunctions and you may want to use some more than once.

so, but, as, since, until, after, and, although, because, while, if, unless, or, when

Yasmin had never seen the point of football .... she went to see Arsenal play Manchester United. Dan had been a fan .... he was a baby .... his dad had always taken him to matches. Deepak's dad had a season ticket .... Deepak had been loads of times. So when Dan's team was playing Deepak's team, they invited their friends to come along .... Deepak's dad had extra tickets. Yasmin thought she'd hate it. She'd said she wouldn't go .... she could take a rug and her Walkman. At first, she couldn't understand what was happening .... was almost deafened by the noise .... once she realised which team was which she started to enjoy it and was still yelling .... the ref. had blown the half-time whistle. During half-time, she asked loads of questions .... she wanted to get the hang of the rules. Dan explained .... Deepak got some chips. .... it was over, Yasmin was still yelling questions. .... she was exhausted, she'd become a real fan.

2 Now write sentences of your own, each one including a different conjunction from the list in Exercise 1.

3 Here is the skeleton of a story. Build up these "bones" into a complete "fleshed-out" story. In each sentence, try to include at least one conjunction from the list in Exercise 1. You can add your own ideas to the story too!

John was desperate to have a scooter.
Christmas was months away.
He had spent all his birthday money.
His sister offered to lend him some.
He didn't like to take it.
He did odd jobs to earn cash.
He got very tired.
His homework was late.
He couldn't concentrate.
His teacher rang home to discuss the problem.
The teacher brought John his daughter's old scooter.
John's mum found one in a car boot sale.
John's dad came home with a new one.
John had gone off scooters and gone on to roller boots.
His sister's old ones were a perfect fit.

SENTENCE | Punctuating conversation

By now you are probably pretty good at punctuation. You know all about commas, full stops, exclamation and question marks, speech marks and even apostrophes. (See pages 18–19 if you're still unsure!) But how confident are you about punctuating conversation?

How to do it ...

Let's remind ourselves of the main rules of punctuating conversation:

a) If you **open** speech marks, you must remember to **close** them again.

b) All speech has some punctuation when it ends – in addition to the speech marks. For example, if a speech is interrupted by a *he said* or a *whispered Yasmin*, it must have a comma, exclamation or question mark **after** what is said, e.g. "I'm sure I saw a mouse," gasped John, "coming out of the cupboard."

c) As you can see in the sentence in (b), you also need a comma **before** the speech continues, i.e. after the *he said* or *whispered Yasmin*. Any interruption to a speech needs punctuation **before and after**.

d) Each new speaker starts on a new indented line, i.e. moved in slightly from the margin. A "new speaker" is whoever did not say the last bit of speech.

The conversation below shows these rules in practice:

"I require," announced Mrs Chinwicket to the owner of the Grimley Pop-In Shop, "ten metres of green string and some frozen peas."

"No problem, love," replied Mr Robinski.

"I also need four large pineapples, some silver ink, a sponge, three black lightbulbs and a small piece of garlic-scented soap," continued Mrs Chinwicket.

"I'll have to get on my steps for the sponge," explained Mr Robinski as he pulled out the ladder, "and I think we might be out of pineapples, but I'm sure they'll be in later."

"The pineapples are essential," said Mrs Chinwicket, sternly. "I cannot possibly wait. The only possible substitute would be emu's eggs, but I expect you're out of those too."

"Emu's eggs? No worries," replied Mr Robinski, cheerily. "We've some nice fresh ones just in."

Look carefully at how passages of conversation are punctuated in any of your own novels. If you find it difficult, ask an adult to copy out some conversation from a book – leaving out the punctuation – and see if you can put it back in correctly.

Sometimes you may be asked to write a play, a scene from a play or an interview. These are also conversations, but they are set out differently from conversation in the context of a story. In these cases, the characters' names are placed on the left-hand side of the page, and the speech is set on the right-hand side – occupying about ¾ of the width of the page. NB Speech marks are not used when a conversation is set out like this.

"If you are getting your commas and full-stops wrong, it means you are not getting your thought right and your mind is muddled."

The Observer, 23 October 1938

Exercises

Now practise!

---

1   The following passage is a conversation between two people. It has no punctuation except for capital letters, dashes and apostrophes. Write it out again, adding speech marks, commas, exclamation and question marks and full stops. Remember to start a new indented line with a capital letter each time the speaker changes.

I'm a bit concerned about Yasmin said Mrs Ali to her teacher Miss Harridan What's the problem asked Miss Harridan I have noticed that she hasn't been concentrating so well lately That's exactly it exclaimed Mrs Ali she can't think about anything other than football She's up at six doing her training exercises waking up the whole house Oh dear sympathised Miss Harridan how annoying And she reads nothing but football magazines went on Mrs Ali Her room is papered with footballers – ugly great things they are too – and now she's joined the Grimley Girls Team she brings home pounds of mud every Saturday and walks it round the house Well I do understand said Miss Harridan and that does explain why her last homework with the title My Ambition was all about captaining the National Women's Football Team What can I do wailed Mrs Ali I want her to think about Maths and Science and History and French Leave it to me advised Miss Harridan I'll have a word with her when I take them to the Fulham v Blackburn match on Saturday I can't wait

64

---

2   Write a conversation of your own or choose one of the following titles:

John and Deepak planning a party
Miss Harridan discussing a match with Mr Thresher
Two dinosaurs meeting over lunch
Neelam persuading her mother to allow her to go to a sleepover
An argument
A confession
John and Deepak after the party
Mr Robinski (the shopkeeper) ordering supplies over the phone

3   Remember that plays, scenes and interviews are written without speech marks. Try writing the following in that way.

   a) A scene in which Yasmin and Dan are trying to explain the pleasures of football to John

   b) An interview between Neelam and her grandfather who has had a most unusual life

   c) An interview between Miss Harridan and the Head Teacher of Trembly High School, near Grimley, after Miss Harridan has applied for a job there

4

68
TOTAL

31

SENTENCE | Organising paragraphs

What is a paragraph? You know by now that it is a group of sentences and that, every now and then, you're supposed to start a new one. But when? Are paragraphs any more than just bunches of sentences? The answer is a definite **yes**. Paragraphing is a useful tool for controlling a story or an argument and for moving it along.

How to do it ...

Here are a few points to remember:

a) A sentence is like a box that contains one idea. A second idea – even if related to the first idea – needs its own box: a new sentence. A third idea – even if it relates to the first and second – needs its own box too: another sentence. All these boxes – and there may be four or five more – need to be put together into a suitcase: a **paragraph**. The suitcase contains all the boxes that belong together. The paragraph contains all the ideas that have something to do with each other. Then, either your argument will take a different turn or something different will happen in your story. This is your cue to start a new paragraph.

b) Paragraphing is helpful in that it allows you to show that you are, for example, changing the time of day or the place in your story or maybe introducing a new character. You may be looking at an argument in a different way. You may want to compare, to present a different view of something, or to bring in new information. In other words, it is both a way for you to organise your material and a helpful indication to the reader that something is changing.

c) A story, description or argument is more interesting if the paragraphs are of different lengths. If a point in an argument is an important one but doesn't need long explanations or if a moment in a story is a big and exciting moment, don't be afraid of putting it in a sentence – and a paragraph – on its own. This can be quite a powerful technique and one much used by journalists. Use it – but not too often!

Look at some different kinds of writing. Start with a novel of your own. How has the writer chosen to set out the story? Are the paragraphs long or short? Do they vary? How much of the book is conversation? Do the same with an adult's book. Is it much the same? How about non-fiction – especially the kind without pictures. There will probably not be any conversation, but how has the writer organised the material? Look at newspapers. Choose two or three different kinds, including one tabloid (the smaller ones) and one broadsheet (the larger ones). What do you notice? Try to compare, for example, the sports reporting.

Finally, look at letters. In newspapers, letters are often shortened and the paragraphing taken out for reasons of space. But what about letters that you or your parents receive? Ask an adult if you can look at some printed letters to see how the paragraphing works.

Look to the Paragraphs and the Argument will take care of itself.

Proverb

Exercises

Now practise!

1   The following passage should be set out in four paragraphs. Read it carefully and mark where the new paragraphs should start.

I wish to apply for the post of English Teacher and Head of Year in Trembly High School. I enclose my curriculum vitae and the application form. I have taught English and games at Grimley High School for four years and now feel ready for a change and more responsibility. While at Grimley High I have taught English throughout the school, introducing a new syllabus to Years 8 and 9. I have also taught netball, rounders and hockey and introduced football as a girls' activity. Grimley now has a very successful girls' football team which, last year, won the County Championship. Outside school I enjoy cookery and mountaineering. Last year I went on a walking tour of the Andes mountain range during which I collected a number of interesting local recipes. In my spare time I am writing a book about Andean breakfasts. It may be of interest to Trembly High that I have qualifications in First Aid, life-saving, operating a fire engine, parachuting, deep sea rescue and bomb disposal – all of which have been useful at Grimley High. I would like to come to Trembly High to broaden my experience.

3

2   **Story**

Choose one of the following titles and write a story, taking care to paragraph at appropriate stages:

The Train Journey   *Going to the Doctor*

3   **Argument**

Discuss the following topic, taking care to start a new paragraph at each new point or stage in your argument:

Is school uniform a good thing?

4   **Description**

Imagine you are a beetle who has been shut in the family's fridge. Describe your journey around the fridge – in and out of various containers, trays, foods, liquids and so on. Have fun imagining what it would all feel like, what the pleasures and perils might be – and remember to use paragraphs to help the reader see the beetle's progress. (This is also a most useful and enjoyable exercise for the writing practice described on page 69.)

5   **Letter**

Write a letter to your local newspaper explaining why you feel Grimley High School should be pulled down and a new school built. You may write as a pupil, a teacher, a parent or a local resident, but remember to use paragraphs to help develop your argument.

4

7
TOTAL

Read carefully the following article from the *Grimley Gazette* and answer the questions below.

Tram Trouble

Local residents are up in arms over controversial plans to build a new tram-line through Grimley. Traffic congestion is so great a problem that an average journey down Grimley High Street at peak times now takes 17 minutes, compared with 6 minutes ten years ago. The drive through Grimley, as everyone agrees, is no longer a pleasure. Pedestrians and cyclists have praised the tram scheme. "Cars and lorries have just taken over," said Ivor Bell, spokesperson for Grimley Cyclists, "a tram's just what Grimley needs." Local shopkeepers take a different view. "We don't want a tram which has no stopping places and which whizzes through Grimley High Street," said Chris P. Bunn, of Bunn's Bakery. "We depend on the passing trade, people jumping out of their cars to pick up a bit of shopping. You can't jump off a tram." Lee Fee-Rhode, local home-owner, agrees. "The tram scheme would mean diverting other traffic along side streets where people live. I don't want great lorries puffing down my road, polluting the air. Traffic should stay on Grimley High Street, where it belongs." Local council official, Hope Lesse, who is in charge of transport, has the task of settling the matter. "We just want to do the best for Grimley," she said, clearly feeling the strain. "The scheme is going along on the right lines but, frankly, all this fuss is sending me off the rails."

1 How many prepositional phrases are in the article?

2 All the sentences in the passage have main clauses, of course. Can you find:

    a) 4 sentences composed of only 1 clause?

    b) 2 subordinate adjectival clauses?

    c) 2 subordinate adverbial clauses?

3 Find 2 coordinating conjunctions.

4 The article above is written as one paragraph – like much journalism.

    a) Take all the pieces of speech in the article and write them out as if it were a conversation. Remember to start a new line for each speaker.

    b) Now write it out as if it were a scene from a play. You may like to carry on the argument about the tram and turn it into a little play!

5 Grimley is holding a public meeting to discuss the tram question. Imagine that you are one of the people quoted in the article and write the speech you will make at the meeting. You should write 3 or 4 paragraphs, using the paragraphs to develop your argument, bringing in new points.

35

TEXT - Reading | Newspapers

Much work in English depends on understanding what you read and being able to answer questions about it. Just think of how many different types of writing you read in an ordinary day – newspapers, magazines, advertisements, instructions, lists, stories, descriptions, recipes, factual accounts, poems, conversations, notices, play scenes, to name but a few! This section looks at some of these in ways that will help you get the most out of them.

How to do it ...

News reports tend not to waste words. They give facts, they quote comments from people who are interviewed, they provide information – in more or less detail, depending on which newspaper they appear in and what is being reported – and they express opinion. Some newspapers present the news in a much more sensational way than others. This means that they like to stir up the feelings of their readers. They do this with startling headlines, more and larger photographs, and in their choice of stories. If you look at the main newspapers in England and Wales, you will find that the stories that make the front pages of *The Independent, The Guardian, The Times* and *The Telegraph* are very often quite different to those that make the front pages of *The Sun* and *The Mirror*, or the same story might be treated in very different ways. *The Express* and *The Daily Mail* may make yet different choices for their front pages. It takes something very important for them all to feature the same event. Check this out next time you visit a newsagent. Below is an example of how differently two newspapers might treat the same story.

Judge frees "blameless" driver

A man who accidentally ran over a dog that ran into the road after its owner lost control of it, was cleared of careless driving by the courts today. Mike Simpson of Grimley Park expressed his relief at the judge's decision and his regret at what had happened. "I feel very sad for the family," he said, "but there was nothing I could do. Now I just want to put this behind me."

DOG-KILLER IN COURTROOM DRAMA

Dog-killer, Michael Simpson, walked free yesterday after Judge Ron Cooper (78) cleared him of the deliberate slaughter of Sparky, a 1-year-old spaniel. Sparky was the treasured pet of twins, Lucy and Oliver Drake (4). According to their mother, Jane (23), the twins are devastated by Sparky's death. "They just keep on crying and can't understand that Sparky isn't coming back. Telling them was the hardest thing I've ever done." Jane is livid with the courts that have let her children down. "That man is evil," she claims, "and the judge doesn't care. I've no faith in the criminal justice system. Something should be done to put people like Simpson behind bars. Whose dog will be next? That's what I want to know."

"A good newspaper, I suppose, is a nation talking to itself."

Arthur Miller (playwright)

Exercises

Now practise!

BOY, 10, MAKES "A" LEVEL HISTORY

*A 10-year-old boy has made academic history by gaining six GCSEs and 1 A level with a B grade in Mathematics, it was **revealed** yesterday. Brilliant Peter Fisher, who attends Trembly High School, Trembly, is the youngest ever pupil to **achieve** so highly. Proud Headmaster, Derek Malcolm, said, "Peter is a gifted boy and very hard-working. He wanted to have a go and we were happy to help." Peter's mum and dad, Nick Fisher and Liz Oliver, were celebrating with him yesterday after they got the news. "He's always been bright," said Liz, "now we want him to relax and enjoy the rest of the summer." Not one to sit back and bask in glory, Peter plans to retake the Maths next term to see if he can get an A grade. But the ten-year-old is **modest** about his achievements so far. "It's no big deal," he said, "you just have to want to do it."*

*Not everyone is so impressed by Peter's success. "Why take important exams so early?" questions Miss Elizabeth Way, Head Teacher of **neighbouring** Grimley High (heavily **criticised** in a recent Inspection). "It just causes problems for the teachers and leaves the child with nothing to do after the exams. What will Peter do in Maths lessons after he's got his A level? Slow, steady learning at the same time as everyone else is much better. Peter and his parents are just **ambitious** and want to show off." Popular Head of Trembly, Derek Malcolm, disagrees. "Children need to learn at their own pace. Peter learns very quickly indeed. Ideally, we would be able to teach everyone **individually** so they would all learn at their own speed." Sadly, given the **current** teacher **shortage**, it seems likely to be a long time before this wonderful **vision** becomes a reality.*

1   Answer these questions about this newspaper report:

   a) What does "made academic history" mean?

   b) Give two words of your own which describe the attitude of Derek Malcolm to Peter.

   c) Is Peter satisfied with his results? How do you know?

   d) The Head of Grimley High is less enthusiastic. Give three of her objections.

   e) Derek Malcolm suggests a different way of teaching. What problem does this pose?

   f) Do you feel that the journalist who wrote this report has an opinion of his or her own? What evidence is there for this?

2   What are your own views on Peter's achievement? Write 3 or 4 sentences giving your opinion.

3   Peter himself says very little in this article. Write an interview with him – either as a conversation or like a play scene (see page 30). You might like to ask him, for example, how he finds time for his work, whether it means giving up other activities, what else he likes doing, and so on.

3

3
TOTAL

TEXT - Reading | First person? Third person?

First person narrative means a piece of writing written as if in the narrator's own voice. *Third person narrative* means a narrative written from the perspective of "he", "she" and "they" rather than "I".

How to do it ...

First person narrative

The writer uses "I" all the way through to tell the story. The writing may be fact or fiction, or a mixture of the two. Autobiographies, diaries, journals and letters are written in this form. Many stories are also written this way. Have a check through your own novels (story books) to see which are written from the "I" point of view – the **first person**. Had you noticed before whether the writer uses "he", "she" and "they" or "I" and "me"? Often it is something we accept without thinking. Do you prefer one approach to the other?

First person writing allows the writer to communicate directly with the reader. The writer can describe his or her own experiences in a way that enables the reader to feel very closely and intimately involved. Can you think of examples of this from your own reading? Of course, a first person account, whether fact or fiction, is written very definitely from only one point of view. Another narrator might describe the same events very differently. A good example of this can be found in journalism (see page 36). Imagine how differently reporters from two warring countries might report a battle!

Third person narrative

Biographies are written in this form, as are historical accounts that attempt to give a balanced picture of events. Although many stories are written using the first person, probably most are still written in the **third person**. The great advantage of this approach is that it enables the writer to be everywhere, know everything, see into the minds and feelings of all the characters, not just the main one, in a way that a first person narrator cannot. It is generally less personal – a third person narrator is writing about the characters rather than speaking through one of them.

We depend on journalists and historians for a fair and balanced presentation of facts – although their own views and personal feelings will always have some influence on how they write. Some of our greatest ever writers of fiction manage to conceal their own sympathies and attitudes and treat all of their characters with the same fairness and insight. Shakespeare and the great Russian novelist Tolstoy are good examples of this. Look through your own books or library books to see what kind of attitude writers take towards their characters. Can you find any stories in which the writer simply presents the events and the characters, without revealing their thoughts to the reader?

On the next page you will read two contrasting accounts, one in the first person and one in the third person. This should help you become more aware of the two ways of telling a story.

Answers | Exercises

Most of the exercises and questions in this book do not have right/wrong answers. Consequently, in most cases, the answers given here only give guidance. You will find, in these pages, suggestions for answers to some of the exercises that are more likely to need such guidance. Otherwise – if you have read the book carefully, you should be able to decide for yourself about the quality of what you have written. And, in the last resort, common sense is an invaluable tool!

Page 7
Exercise 1
peace, which, knew, new, witch, piece, blue, blew

Page 7
Exercise 2
a) *counsellor*   b) *practise*
c) *discrete*   d) *discreet*
e) *complement* f) *practice*
g) *councillor* h) *compliment*

Page 7
Exercise 3
The correct spellings are: *business, biscuits, recipes, delicious, decide, tongue, probably, especially, finally, favourite, excitedly, disappeared*

Page 9
Exercise 1
The following are some suggested adverbs, but there are hundreds more to choose from: *endlessly, lovingly, thoroughly, lavishly, gingerly, carefully, briefly, guiltily, meticulously*

Page 9
Exercise 2
Here are some possible answers: *always, rarely, occasionally, usually, sometimes, frequently, never, often, infrequently*

Page 11
Exercise 1
disappointed, disallowed, disable, disbelieve, disconnect, dishonest, disloyal, disservice, disobey, dissimilar

Page 11
Exercise 2
truly, wisely, sleepily, nicely, wonderfully,

humbly, actually, healthily, usually, cheerily

Page 11
Exercise 3
sitting, patting, stopped, stunned, diving, wading, dripping, blamed, rubbed, getting, dragged, dropped, whiling, gazing

Page 13
Exercise 1
under, with, in, for, down, to, between, out, above, through, into, around, along, of, before, up, with

Page 15
Exercise 2
Some of the possible combinations are:
fit up, fit out, fit in, fit in with....
set up, set down, set out, set off, set to....
call up, call out, call on, call over, call around....
get up, get down, get out, get off, get around to, get up to, get away from....
hold on, hold up, hold out, hold over, hold to....
pay up, pay out, pay in, pay into....

Page 18
Exercise 1
isn't, you're, she's, they'll, Mrs Chinwicket's, we'd, can't, should've, don't, we're, would've, aren't, you've, he'll, could've, weren't, wouldn't, I'm, they're, she's, I'd

Page 18
Exercise 2
Because these give so much trouble, these examples are given in full. See how they follow the rule on page 18:

the rabbit's ears, the men's team, the spiders' webs, the boy's boots, the model's hats, Thomas's book, the artists' work, the bees' hive, the boys' pictures, the children's party, the ladies' home, the girl's clothes

Page 19
Exercise 3

What's the new boy's name, I wonder? He's looking as though he's lost his way and his backpack's splitting its sides with all the new books. He's sitting on Deepak's table but he's in Yasmin's group for Maths and John's for English. I've got him for Mr Snapperchild's lesson and he'll need warning about that. He's left his coat in the boys' cloakroom but his trainers are in the teachers' lockers and they won't like that. He looks as if he'd be quite fun so I'll see if he'll sit next to me for Ms Moss's class and maybe it'll be less boring than usual. Then it's the Snapperchild and you're never really prepared for that! I wonder whose bus he goes home on?

Page 19
Exercise 4

(Dan's /Dans) lost his cat. (Dan's /Dans) (cat's /cats) name is Goblin. (Its /It's) jet black and has blue eyes and (it's /its) never been any good at finding (it's/its) way home. Dan put up a notice in Mrs (Dass/Das's) window but (no-ones/no-one's) rung up so far. Goblin disappeared once before and the caretaker found him in the (boys'/boy's) cloakroom at the sports pitch. I don't think (cats' /cat's) memories can be very good, or maybe they just like a change now and then.

Page 21 – Section practice

a) *then*, *before* and *early* are adverbs of time; *around*, *here* and *there* are adverbs of place
b) *show*
c) 14 apostrophes show missed letters, 3 show belonging (teachers', Harridan's, friend's)
d) *patiently*
e) separate is the correct spelling
f) Use the dictionary!
g) Use the dictionary!
h) You should find at least 20 more

Page 23
Exercise 1

a) i) in my class, ii) about football
b) before tea
c) i) in Grimley Road, ii) of all kinds
d) of Grimley Junior School
e) i) *of the Baskervilles*, ii) by Sir Arthur Conan Doyle
f) i) behind the hall, ii) into the corridor
g) i) with maple syrup, ii) for tea

Page 23
Exercise 2

For example: a) *down the street*; b) *over there*; c) *on Friday*; d) *in my class*; e) *to the show*; f) *on the pitch*; g) *in the high street, for sale*

Page 25
Exercise 1

a) I like stations
b) Trains sometimes go through very long tunnels
c) The guard was very knowledgeable about the area
d) The day will be the best day of my life
e) Hotel managers are quite used to tourists
f) The café was very crowded

Page 25
Exercise 2

a) John ate his beans, which were cold, and he dropped the plate, which broke.
[4 clauses: 2 main, 2 subordinate adjectival]
b) Deepak, who loves pizzas with different toppings, makes his own at home.
[2 clauses: 1 main, 1 subordinate adjectival]
c) Mr Snapperchild was not pleased with the girls who had filled his wellies with sand.
[2 clauses: 1 main, 1 subordinate adjectival]
d) Dan could go to Russia or he might fly to Venezuela, where he has relations.
[3 clauses: 2 main, 1 subordinate adjectival]
e) Ijah raced round the corner and he charged up the road, which was very icy, and he leapfrogged the railings and he slid into the duckpond. [5 clauses: 4 main, 1 subordinate adjectival]
f) My auntie, who loves animals, has six cats, four canaries, an Alsatian, a rabbit and seven gerbils. [2 clauses: 1 main, 1 subordinate adjectival]

Page 27
Exercise 1

are making, have poured, are melting, made, ate, watched, is greasing, mixes, adores, says, won't eat, plans, licks, is wiping, licks, fills

Page 27
Exercise 2

(finite verbs are shown with double underlining for clarity)

Ijah is very good at tree houses. He went into the woods the day after school had broken up. Deepak and John went too so that Ijah could teach them about tree house techniques. Because it was winter, their hands got very cold and they had to wear gloves. John worked as hard as he could. He carried branches until his back ached. Ijah stacked them up where they were out of the wind. Although the boys worked hard all day, the tree house was still only a pile of branches by sunset. After they had worked for three whole days, they held a tree house-warming party.

Page 29
Exercise 1

Here are some possible answers:
until, since, because, so, since, unless, and, but, after, because, while, when, although

Page 31
Exercise 1

"I'm a bit concerned about Yasmin," said Mrs Ali to her teacher, Miss Harridan.

"What's the problem?" asked Miss Harridan, "I have noticed that she hasn't been concentrating so well lately."

"That's exactly it!" exclaimed Mrs Ali. "She can't think about anything other than football. She's up at six doing her training exercises, waking up the whole house!"

"Oh dear," sympathised Miss Harridan, "how annoying!"

"And she reads nothing but football magazines," went on Mrs Ali. "Her room is papered with footballers – ugly great things they are too – and, now she's joined the Grimley Girls Team, she brings home pounds of mud every Saturday and walks it round the house."

"Well, I do understand," said Miss Harridan, "and that does explain why her last homework, with the title 'My Ambition', was all about captaining the National Women's Football Team."

"What can I do?" wailed Mrs Ali. "I want her to think about Maths and Science and History and French."

"Leave it to me," advised Miss Harridan. "I'll have a word with her when I take them to the Fulham v Blackburn match on Saturday. I can't wait!"

Page 33
Exercise 1

The paragraphs (which are really too short but are here just to give you the idea) should end at: *responsibility*, *Championship*, *breakfasts*, and *experience*

Page 35 – Section practice

The words in CAPITALS are prepositional phrases. All the underlined sentences only have one clause (remember that participles are not finite verbs). All the clauses in *italics* are subordinate adjectival clauses. The clauses in **bold** are subordinate adverbial ones. "And" and "but" are coordinating conjunctions.

Local residents are 1. UP IN ARMS 2. OVER CONTROVERSIAL PLANS to build a new tram-line THROUGH GRIMLEY. Traffic congestion is so great a problem **that an average journey** 1. **DOWN GRIMLEY HIGH STREET 2. AT PEAK TIMES now takes 17 minutes**, compared with 6 minutes ten years ago. The drive THROUGH GRIMLEY, **as everyone agrees**, is no longer a pleasure. Pedestrians and cyclists have praised the tram scheme. "Cars and lorries have just taken over," said Ivor Bell, spokesperson FOR GRIMLEY CYCLISTS, "a tram's just *what Grimley needs*." Local shopkeepers take a different view. "We don't want a tram *which has no stopping places* and *which whizzes THROUGH GRIMLEY HIGH STREET*," said Chris P. Bunn, OF BUNN'S BAKERY. "We depend ON THE PASSING TRADE, people jumping OUT OF THEIR CARS to pick UP A BIT OF SHOPPING. You can't jump OFF A TRAM. Lee Fee-Rhode, local

Answers

home-owner, agrees. "The tram scheme would mean diverting other traffic ALONG SIDE STREETS *where people live*. I don't want great lorries puffing DOWN MY ROAD, polluting the air. Traffic should stay ON GRIMLEY HIGH STREET, **where it belongs**." Local council official, Hope Lesse, *who is* 1. *IN CHARGE* 2. *OF TRANSPORT*, has the task OF SETTLING THE MATTER. "We just want to do the best FOR GRIMLEY," she said, clearly feeling the strain. "The scheme is going along ON THE RIGHT LINES but, frankly, all this fuss is sending me OFF THE RAILS."

For guidance in assessing how well the work for questions 4 and 5 has been completed, refer to the sections on conversation (pages 30–31) and organising paragraphs (pages 32–33).

It would not be possible here to give "answers" to most of the exercises or questions in Sections 3 and 4. Common sense and a careful reading of the pages preceding each exercise ought to help and a friendly adult might be of use too, if you have one handy! While there may not be right or wrong answers, these exercises are vital for preparing children for the expectations of Secondary School.

Answers | Test Papers

Paper One

1

> There had been no snow for years. Most of the children had never seen it before so they couldn't concentrate in lessons once it began. Ijah missed the beginning and, at first, he wasn't sure what it was. Finally, the teacher let them go outside. However, she said very firmly, "No snow down people's necks, everyone. I don't want any accidents." Ijah found Dan.
>
> "It's such a surprise," he said. "We didn't ever have snow in Jamaica." Dan agreed.
>
> "It's pretty unusual and it's beautiful." They met Neelam, who looked terrified.
>
> "It's dangerous!" she complained. "It's extremely slippery and horrible and you can't walk properly." Dan picked up some snow and put it on his tongue.
>
> "Mmm! Delicious!" he said. "Look over there! Who is it?"
>
> "Where?" asked Neelam. "Oh, it's John! Don't you recognise him?" John had got a hat pulled down over his eyes.
>
> "I'd be embarrassed to go out like that," said Ijah.
>
> "You're just jealous!" said Dan. "Come on," he decided, "it's time to make a mountain."

2   See pages 56-57 for guidance in assessing your answers for question 2.

Paper Two

a) The comparison is between the attractive, safe appearance of the mountain on days when the weather is good and its threatening, perilous nature when the weather is bad.
b) The Irish Sea
c) They had taken proper precautions and were sensibly equipped.
d) He wanted to give them some time on their own, he wanted to make some soup and he wanted to finish an article.
e) He should have been as he had lived there for twenty years and must have known it was changeable.
f) First some annoyance that their walk should be spoiled, then worry and then, as time went on, serious anxiety for their safety.
g) *on bright, warm days; over the years; over the hilltops; on their own, etc....*
h) i) *It was bright and clear.*
   ii) *when Mike and Jane set off that morning* or *When the phone rang at half past four*
   iii) *I'd expected them back for lunch, but at two I ate my soup alone.*
i) Refer to pages 30, 42, and 43 to check your answer.

Paper Three

For guidance in assessing how well the work in this section has been planned and written, refer to the sections on planning (pages 62–63), fleshing out a story (pages 64–67) and writing non-fiction (pages 56–61). There are no right or wrong answers, but the exercise is vital for preparing children for the expectations of Secondary School.

Exercises

Now practise!

Here are two extracts. Each comes from a different story. Each passage deals with having to say goodbye. Read both of them carefully and answer the questions below.

---

i   **Saying Goodbye**

Lauren was drawing on a piece of white paper on the kitchen table. She had laid out her felt-tipped pens and was drawing a horse. Mum was in and out with articles of Dad's clean clothing. She seemed to need to bustle about. Upstairs, Simon was chatting to Dad, watching him pack. Lauren gave her horse a yellow mane, a big, wild one, flaring out in the wind. Mum came in again. Lauren didn't look up. She bent further over her page, wondering how she could draw wind. Upstairs, Dad was zipping his case. Lauren could hear his voice and his short laugh after something Simon said. Then feet on the stairs. Lauren gripped her pen and pressed it hard into the page. She felt her face getting hot and her eyes began to smart.

---

ii   **Saying Goodbye**

No-one could have wanted to go on that school trip more than me. Mum and I had never been abroad – there'd never been the money for it and holidays had been sharing a caravan near the beach in Wales with my cousins – whatever the weather. A week in France with my mates, even if the teachers were there too, giving us work, well, it was the best thing I could think of. That was until I was packing my bag. Mum brought in my tee-shirts, my jeans, underwear. She kept checking I'd got my tooth-brush, camera, asthma inhaler, passport – everything I'd packed the night before while she watched! It was driving me mad. Then I caught sight of her face. She suddenly looked much older. And I could see what she was thinking. She'd not been without me since I was born. Now she would be alone for the first time in eleven years.

---

a)   Which passage is written in the first person and which in the third person?

b)   In passage (i), something is about to happen. Can you say what it is?

c)   How are Simon, Mum and Lauren reacting to this?

d)   How do you think Lauren feels about what is happening? What clues are there?

e)   In passage (ii), we learn some facts about the first person narrator. (His name is Alan.) Give two of them.

f)   What impression do you get of Alan's personality?

g)   Explain the change that takes place in Alan's state of mind when he sees his Mum's face. Can you explain why this happens?

h)   Passage (i) is written in the third person and passage (ii) is in the first person. Does one passage make you feel more involved than the other? If so, why?

i)   Rewrite the two passages. Write the first one as though you are Lauren and write the second one as a third person narrator.

9

9
TOTAL

TEXT – READING | Fiction

Reading fiction is one of the most popular activities engaged in by adults and children. However much time people spend at the cinema, watching TV or on their computers, they still read masses of books! In fact, perhaps surprisingly, sales of books, especially of fiction, are rising rather than falling – not at all what people predicted when computers began to be popular!

How to do it ...

Understanding, *comprehending*, what you read is not always simple, and you will have learned scanning and skimming techniques to help you identify key words and phrases. It is seldom necessary to know every word in a passage to understand its meaning. Often you can make sensible guesses about a word from the words that surround it – its *context*.

However, have you ever read a book and got to the end and wondered what it was all about? This may be because you skipped over an important event or a few words and just lost the thread. While scanning, skimming and guessing are all important techniques, they can be of limited help when reading fiction. Sometimes you have to read carefully because the scene being described is important and you need to be able to *visualise* it, i.e. see it in your own mind's eye, in order to understand what is going on at that point in the story. The passage on page 41 is an example of this. Often you also need to be able to read *between the lines* – this means that something about the characters or their situation may not be explained plainly and it's left up to you to work it out from the information given. Passage (i) on page 39 is a good example of this. Nowhere does it *say* that Lauren was unhappy but I bet you knew she was! This is where you need to read *slowly*, *carefully* and *thoughtfully*. Sometimes you have to learn a lot about characters, not from what the narrator says about them but from what they say themselves. On page 43 you will find an example of this. Again, you need to read carefully to pick up on these words and phrases that, while only brief, give you valuable information.

At school you are often asked to read a passage and then answer questions. Some of the questions will be straightforward but others require careful study of the passage – what is *actually* said, not what you *think* was said! Start to learn to read *in detail* and *with care* now and you will find future English language work much easier.

On the next page you will find part of a story that may well challenge you, followed by questions. Go slowly. You can do it!

"The good ended happily and the bad unhappily. That is what fiction means."

Oscar Wilde (Is it true?)

Exercises

Now practise!

Starfish rescue

Holly looked around. Granny was there, settling herself in a dip in the stones and unfolding her newspaper. Holly thought of calling to ask if she might take off her shoes but Granny wouldn't hear over the blow of the wind. So she ran back to where the stones began and quickly pulled off her trainers and socks. She stood on the cold, wet sand. If you stood for a minute or two, the sand became wobbly under your feet. She rolled up the ends of her jeans. Then she noticed the breakwater.

It was a huge, lumpy, cracked and broken wall, stretching all the way from the stones down to the sea. It looked like a knobbly finger, black and warty. She walked towards it. It was made of big stones set in concrete and it seemed to be covered in a kind of shiny crust. When she got close, she could see that the crust was made up of thousands and thousands of black mussel shells stuck to the wall in stiff, bristling crowds. Each shell had tinier white shells stuck on it. Between them, frills of brown and green seaweed flickered in the wind.

Holly tried to pull one mussel off the wall and grazed her fingers on the gritty shell. She tried another and it came away with a suck and a crunch. It was closed tight like an eyelid – like an eye turned to stone, she thought. She dropped it into the little pool.

There were lots of little hollows and pools under the breakwater. Mussels clung to the ceilings while the water ran down in streams to the sea. Holly suddenly noticed a huge starfish, beached on the edge of one of the little pools. It was brick-coloured and looked rather dried up. She bent to stare at it. Under its five triangular points, it had tiny, thin white tentacles like little tubes. They were waving, very slightly, in the shallow trickle of water.

"Are you dead?" wondered Holly. The tentacles still moved. She stood up and looked for something to poke it with. There was a long, thin, black shell sticking up from under the breakwater. She leaned over and wrenched it up. The starfish was still. She eased the black shell under one of its points and watched the tentacles. It hadn't been the water making them move. They waved feebly – all in different directions. "You're not dead," she said, "not quite. Not yet." Gently she pushed the starfish properly into the pool. Sand began to wash over it. "Go on," she said. "Get better."

She stood up. The sea had come a little closer. She padded down to where it rushed over her feet – very cold and tickly. It felt wonderful. She took a great gulp of air and tore down the beach, splashing through tiny waves, wanting to laugh with excitement. The beach was empty and all hers.

---

a) Explain in your own words why Holly doesn't ask her granny whether she can take off her shoes.

b) Why do you think Holly rolled up her jeans?

c) In your own words, carefully describe the breakwater.

d) Give three reasons why Holly thought the starfish might be dead.

e) How did she rescue the starfish?

f) Explain fully and in your own words how Holly felt when the sea reached her.

g) This passage looks very closely at things. Choose two examples of details you like and explain the reasons why.

`10`

41

TEXT – READING | Conversation

Open one of your own novels. Is there a conversation on the page? How much conversation is there in the rest of the book? How about a different book? What about an adult's book? Some novels are largely composed of conversation. Others rely far more on narrative. It's interesting to compare how and how much different writers use conversation.

How to do it ...

Conversation is a very important tool for a writer for a number of reasons:

a) It is a way of giving information rapidly and concisely.

b) It conveys a sense of the characters' personalities, as everyone talks in their own way.

c) It contributes to our knowledge of the characters' relationships.

d) It gives a sense of *immediacy*, i.e. that something is happening *while* you read it.

e) It can be dramatic – like a scene from a play.

f) It breaks up lengthy passages of description or narrative.

Read the following passage carefully and see if you can find examples of the above points.

Joe has managed to escape from his kidnappers. He has spent two days lost in a huge forest, trying to find his way out. Finally he smells smoke and follows the scent:

> It was getting harder to walk and Joe's grazed knee was throbbing. Still, that faint scent of smoke drew him on. His eyes hunted for a brightening between the trees. Sometime, there must be an end to the forest. He stumbled on. Suddenly, the smoke was harsh and strong. Voices. He strained his eyes for movement, colour. Then a loud laugh. A man's laugh – close by. Joe moved on, scanning the ground for anything that might crackle, snap. There, in a clearing, two men by a heavily smoking fire.
>
> "I thought you knew how to make a fire!" jeered one of them. "You, the famous boy scout!" He had long grey shorts and was laughing and coughing all at once. "Some expert!" A great gust of smoke billowed up. The second man, in a yellow rugby shirt, muttered something Joe couldn't hear. He moved closer.
>
> "We'll never cook on that! Unless you want to smoke your sausages!" spluttered the man in shorts.
>
> "It'll be OK, just give it a little time," said rugby shorts, calmly. "Get out some bread and cheese if you're hungry." He gestured at a nearby backpack.
>
> "Hungry? I'm starved!" yelled grey shorts. "You're not getting away with this, Sam. I've heard about the Sam Smith campfire method all the way here and now look at it! If you can! Here! Here's a sausage for you!" He jumped up, grabbed one of the raw sausages and tried to force it into rugby shirt's mouth. They were laughing and yelling and pummelling each other and Joe realised that they were actually not much older than him. Suddenly, the smoke caught the back of his throat.
>
> "Stop it, you idiot," pleaded rugby shirt, mildly.
>
> "Not till you've eaten this sausage!"
>
> Joe bit his lips. But there was nothing he could do. A huge cough burst from his mouth.

Exercises

Now practise!

"There's nothing for it," **announced** *Mum, "we'll have to move house."*

"Over my dead body," **retorted** *Francis. "It's taken me years to get my room sorted. I've just got all my posters in exactly the right positions. No way I'm moving!"*

"I'm sorry, darling, but the house is just too small for us now and it's falling apart. And Olivia must have a bigger room."

"I don't want a bigger room."

"She doesn't want a bigger room. She doesn't need a bigger room. It's her nest. She only comes out when she wants food."

"Well, we can't afford to do all the repairs here. We need a bigger house in a cheaper area and I shall phone the agent tomorrow."

"No-one would want to buy this house!" **exploded** *Francis. "It's a rat-hole. You'd have to be mad to buy it. The bathroom ceiling is still in the bath and the kitchen floor seems to be crawling up behind the fridge. Anyone'd see that!"*

"Oh I don't think so. It'll all look fine with some paper over the worst bits and a little paint and polish."

"Well, Dad won't want to move. Will you Dad? Dad! Dad!! D'you want to move?"

"Sorry, Francis. Were you talking to me?" Dad put down his book.

"This is important, Dad!"

"What is?"

Francis lifted his eyes to the ceiling. "Mum wants us to move house."

"Does she? Oh all right then." He returned to his book.

"That settles it. We've been here far too long. Olivia is beginning to look like a small mole. And she can't keep on having sleepovers on the stairs. She must have a bigger room."

"I don't want a bigger room."

---

1 This extract is almost entirely conversation. However, you may feel that you learn something about the characters' personalities from their conversation. Write a sentence or two about:

    a) Mum

    b) Francis

    c) Olivia

    d) Dad

2 How does the writer make it clear who is talking even when she doesn't add a "said Francis" or similar?

3 Look at the 3 words in **bold** – the few times the writer *does* tell us who is talking. She could just have written "said" in each case. How might this have altered the overall feel of the passage?

4 Try to continue the conversation for another page, maintaining the individual characters' ways of talking.

4

4
TOTAL

TEXT – READING | Persuasion

Much of what we read is designed to persuade us. Through the letter box come letters from political candidates telling us why we should vote for them. Newspapers are full of advertisements tempting us with unbeatable prices on things we find we want. Whole pages invite us to *Join the Army – see The World!* or ask, *Have you got what it takes to be a Policeman?* or tell us that, *No Job is more rewarding than Teaching!* Brochures from travel companies make us long for those sunny beaches and exotic views. Many newspapers also have "Opinion" columns in which the writer presents arguments to convince us of the rightness of his or her opinion on a particular topic.

How to do it ...

Writing to persuade is a highly skilled art. It isn't surprising that successful advertisement writers get very well paid! How is it done? Look through newspapers and magazines for advertisements. Many rely on pictures rather than words – but even a few words can be very powerful with the right picture. It's the same with TV advertisements. Look critically at the advertisements next time you're watching TV. How many words are actually used? How do they relate to what you see? How important are the words, or is what you see all-important? Who would you say the advertisement is aimed at? Does it interest you in the product being advertised? Do you remember the advertisement or the product afterwards? Is the advertisement funny? Attractive? Boring? Incomprehensible?

Targeting persuasion at the right audience and at a time when they are open to being persuaded are key parts of the technique. Look, for example, at the TV advertisements that come up between 4:00 p.m. and 6:00 p.m. They are clearly aimed at a very different audience to those shown later or in the morning. You won't find them advertising beer or fast cars but you *will* see advertisements for stair lifts and toys!

If you are given something to read which is designed to persuade, ask yourself the following questions.

   a) Who is this aimed at?

   b) How much actual language is in it, or is the approach mostly *visual*, i.e. with pictures?

   c) How does it look on the page – eye-catching? Dull? Confusing?

   d) Is it clear and easy to understand or do I need to think about it?

   e) Is it informative? Amusing? Boring? Exciting?

   f) Does it persuade me? Is it successful in what it sets out to do?

Think about how you would set out to persuade someone. Perhaps you want to be allowed to have a dog? go to a sleepover? go out on your own with friends? stay up late? and you need to convince a parent that it's OK. Do you choose a good time? Do you approach it in a way that gets the adult on your side? Have you thought out your arguments before you start? Do you expect to win/lose before you start? Do you get unreasonable? Angry? Rude?! All these things count in any attempt to persuade – whether spoken or written. Some people get so worked up when they try to persuade you of their point of view – see, for example, the very cross letters that sometimes make it into newspapers – that it makes you determined to see things the *other* way!

"The pen is mightier than the sword."

E.G. Bulwer-Lytton

Exercises

Now practise!

Dan's mum, Sonia Edwards, is standing for election to Grimley Council. She has just written her campaign leaflet. Here it is:

Care about Grimley's future? **VOTE SONIA EDWARDS**

Dear Neighbours,
I am standing as your Labour Party candidate for Grimley Park in the forthcoming election and I hope very much to have your support. I have been a resident of Grimley for 14 years and know very well the good and bad points of living in our borough. I feel now that the time has come for me to do something about the things in Grimley that drive us all mad!
Firstly, if elected, I would scrap the daft plan to route a tram down our High Street. The tram would just rattle through our main shopping street without stopping and take away parking space for the shoppers who want to use our shops. It would be disastrous for the small shops in Grimley and just play into the hands of the supermarkets. Secondly, I would raise funds to build a new car park behind the station so *that more people can take the train into the city and more shoppers can leave their cars off the roads. Thirdly, I would campaign to have Grimley High School knocked down so that we can build a new, modern school of which Grimley can be proud! Finally, I want to build an international, world class Sports Centre in Grimley. It's ridiculous that we have to go to Trembly which is over-crowded and two bus rides away. We all need somewhere local which would be a good social centre and which would improve our health. Vote for me if you care about Grimley and a better way of life!*

A campaign leaflet has to persuade potential voters. What chance do you think this one has?

1 Who is this leaflet aimed at?

2 What is your first impression of the leaflet? Do you want to read it?

3 What points do you think Sonia is trying convey in the first paragraph? Does she do it successfully?

4 Which two of the following words best describe the language Sonia uses in the leaflet as a whole: a) official b) boring c) friendly d) serious e) enthusiastic f) complicated?

5 Do you think voters are likely to agree with her four plans? Give your own views.

6 Do you think voters who read Sonia's leaflet would be likely to vote for her?

7 Choose one of Sonia's plans and write a letter to the Grimley Gazette arguing strongly against the plan. Give all your reasons.

8 Write your own campaign leaflet saying what you would change in your area.

8

8
TOTAL

TEXT – READING | Poems

Poems can be about anything. They can tell huge stories about voyages or wars, they can be outpourings of love or sorrow, they can be funny, political, thoughtful, religious, descriptive, rude – in short, anything! A good poem can have a powerful effect on a reader and stay in the mind forever. Everyone can remember a bit of a poem they liked at some time.

How to do it ...

Here are some points and questions you should think about when looking at a poem:

1 *What is the poem about*? Often, this is really *the* question – without which none of the other questions make much sense. Does the title help you? Does the poem tell a story? Does it describe a person or a place? Does it capture a moment? A scene? A mood?

2 From whose *point of view* is the poem written?

3 Does the poem create an *atmosphere*? For example creepy, hilarious, sad, scary?

4 *How does the poem work*? Does it use rhyme? If so, how does this help you to enjoy the poem or to learn it?

5 Some poems have an obvious regular *rhythm*, the beat. Does this one? If so, what kind of a rhythm is it? Fast? Slow? Bouncy? Solemn? If not, does it still seem to have a rhythmic feel, even if it isn't regular? How does this help the poem move along?

6 Look at the *words* used in the poem. Are they long words with lots of syllables? Short, simple words? Why do you think the poet chose these kinds of words for this poem?

7 Some poets use the *sound* of words very carefully. For example, long vowels such as *ay, ee, oo* or soft consonants, such as *l, m, n*, can create special effects. In, "the slow drone of the bumble bees murmured among the clover hummocks," you *should* be able to hear a soft humming sound!

8 Some poets like using *comparisons*, sometimes called *metaphors* or *similes*, when one thing is compared to something else. For example, "the new sheet lay like a field of untouched snow" or "the sky was a floor cloth hung out to dry." Are there any in your poem?

9 Finally – and most important – *do you like the poem*? Can you describe your feelings about it and work out why you feel as you do?

Choose a poem from one of your own books or a library book and answer the questions above. Ask yourself these questions in relation to any poems you may be asked to write about in the future or use them as helpful hints if you want to write your own poems!

"Poetry is the opening and closing of a door, leaving those who look through to guess about what is seen during a moment."

Carl Sandburg

Exercises

Now practise!

Attila Takes A Hand

We drive through the gateway,
Get out of the car
And see to our horror
The door is ajar.

"My God! We've been burgled!
It's happened again!
Perhaps they're still in there?
Bad boys? Or tough men?"

But where is Attila?
Where *is* that beast?
We thought the Alsatian
Would scare them at least.

Oh, here is the hero!
And wagging his tail!
Why didn't you give them
The CDs as well?

"Get back to the kitchen!
Guard dog indeed!
No-one so cowardly
Should wear collar and lead!"

Attila slinks out
But then, strangely, lingers
And sniffs by his forepaw
Two fresh human fingers.

© Susan Hamlyn

Read the above poem carefully and then answer the following questions:

1   Can you tell, in two or three sentences, the story of the poem?

2   Through whose eyes is the story told?

3   There is a moment of fear in verse two. Can you explain what it is?

4   The tone of the poem changes in verse four. How would you describe the way this verse might be said?

5   In verse five Attila is accused of being "cowardly"? How fair, by the end of the poem, do you think this is?

6   How easily did you understand this poem and visualise what happens? Can you explain your reasons? Think about the *words* the poet has chosen, the use of a *voice*, the rhyming and use of a regular rhythm, etc.

7   The poem is quite dramatic. How does the poet convey the drama and excitement?

8   Do you like this poem? Can you say why – or why not?

9   Write a story – or a poem of your own – saying what happens on this day from Attila's point of view.

9

9
TOTAL

47

TEXT – READING | Section practice

Read the following passage and answer the questions **as fully as possible**.

Deepak waited. His dad was still working on some figures and he didn't like interruptions. Deepak looked at his watch. He had half an hour till bed-time. It was now or never. "Come on, Dad," he urged, silently. Finally, finally, Dad looked up.

"You want something?"

"Yeah. Please, Dad."

"Well? I've not got all night."

"Well ..." How to start? He'd had it all clear in his head but now it was fading away. "Dad. You know John? You know he's got that new dog?"

"Ye – es? And?" Dad sounded cautious, impatient.

"If I promised I'd take care of it, walk it, feed it, groom it, not be late for school or anything, couldn't I, please ..."

"I'm sorry, Deepak. You know how I feel about dogs."

"But it'd be good practice for being responsible. I could get a scout's badge for looking after it."

"Give it a rest, Deepak."

"And it'd be protection. We wouldn't be burgled if we had a dog. They bark ..."

"I know that."

"And they bite ..." Deepak felt he was losing this argument. "Please, Dad."

1   Who starts the conversation?

2   Do you think Deepak has chosen a good time for this conversation?

3   How well has he prepared his arguments?

4   What impression do you get of Deepak's dad from this conversation?

5   Does he come up with any reasons why Deepak can't have a dog?

6   Do you feel sorry for Deepak by the end of this conversation? Give reasons for your answer.

7   Judging by this conversation, what kind of relationship does Deepak have with his father?

8   This passage is written in the third person. Write Deepak's own account of the conversation (i.e. rewrite it in the first person). You will need to write at least a page.

9   Imagine you want to persuade an adult to allow you to do or have something you want badly. Write the discussion you have, either as a conversation set out like the one above or as a play scene.

10 "Children should be seen and not heard," goes an old saying. Some parents are much more prepared to discuss things than others. Write an "Opinion" article for a newspaper with the headline **Children should be heard too**, in which you discuss this question.

11 Grimley Lost Dogs' Home is short of money. Make a poster – on a computer if you like – which the Home can use to advertise its fund-raising campaign. It should be a combination of pictures and persuasive writing.

11

11
TOTAL

TEXT – WRITING | Reviews

Just as with reading, there are many kinds of *writing*. By your age you'll have written descriptions, stories, letters, factual accounts, poems and many other types of writing. This section is about techniques that will help with your writing of all kinds.

How to do it ...

Why write a book review? There are two main reasons. Firstly, you can help a friend decide whether they want to read the book you're writing about. Secondly, thinking carefully about a book can help you get clearer about your own reaction to it and about why you have that reaction. This, in turn, can help your own writing. It can also help you develop and understand your own tastes so that you know better what books you like and which you'd rather avoid! On the following page you'll find a series of headings under which you can write a paragraph or so about a novel you have recently read. Now, let's explain the headings:

a) What attracted you to the book? A friend's recommendation? You saw it in the library/bookshop/on TV?

b) The title and the cover. Is it a good title for the book? Does it give you a fair impression of the type of book it is? Does it make you want to try it? What about the cover – is it inviting? Off-putting? Dull?

c) What kind of book is it? Is it funny? Exciting? Dramatic? A thriller? Fantasy? A family story? Science fiction? Horror? How would you describe it?

d) How quickly did you feel involved in the story? Did you have to persevere for a while?

e) What about the characters? How real are they? Did you believe in them?

f) Did it hold your interest? How did it do this?

g) What about the ending? Did you guess how it would end? Was it a let-down or a surprise? Was it a good way to end?

h) Would you recommend the book to a friend? If so, why? If not, why not?

Finally, it's not just books that can be reviewed. You can think about the above questions in relation to TV programmes, films, videos, shows, plays – even video games. Take a little time to look through the Reviews or Arts section of a broadsheet (large format) newspaper and see how many different things get reviewed.

"No-one can write a book which children will like unless he writes it for himself first."

A. A. Milne

Exercises

Now practise!

1   Choose a book you've read recently or know well. Then, after referring back to page 50 if you need more details, write a review using the following headings:

   a) Why I chose to read this book

   b) The title and the cover

   c) What type of book is it? Is it a type I normally like?

   d) How quickly did it involve me?

   e) The characters – are they believable, enjoyable?

   f) Was my interest held throughout? How was this achieved?

   g) What kind of ending was it? Did it surprise me? Was it predictable? Disappointing? (Make sure you don't give the ending away!)

   h) Would I recommend it? To anyone?

8

Now think about other things you could recommend to people – or not recommend! How about a TV programme? A film? A video? A show? Or even a place you've been to – a theme park? A zoo? A museum? A holiday resort? Here are some writing exercises:

2   Ask a friend to recommend a TV programme you don't normally see or, perhaps, a video you haven't watched before. Watch it *critically*, noting down any thoughts you have as you watch – or as soon after as you can. Use the points above to help you make your judgements. You will also need to think of the *visual* effects – what you *see* – as well. Look at, for example, close-ups, zooms, the length of each sequence, the amount of dialogue compared to the amount of time you *see* without *hearing* dialogue. Consider, too, the way sound and music are used. Then write a letter – aimed, perhaps, at *The Radio Times* or another TV/film magazine, giving, in detail, your opinion on what you have seen. Set it out in an orderly way as with the book review above. Also take care to set it out as a formal letter (see pages 58–61) if you're not sure.

3   Now think about a place you've visited – perhaps a museum, theme park, holiday resort, park, city farm etc. Write down as much about it as you can remember – or maybe consult a brochure or Web site about it if you can find one. You will need quite a bit of factual information to do this exercise – not just your memories and opinions. Then write a leaflet advertising this place. You will need to provide factual information – where it is, how to get there, what the entrance fee is, opening times, what type of place it is, who it's for, what you can do/see there and so on. (If necessary you can make up some of the details!) This exercise can be done on a computer if you want to – to produce a really professional looking leaflet!

2

10
TOTAL

Although some playwrights write lengthy stage directions about how they want their characters to look, dress, move and speak etc., most do not and rely on the speeches they give their characters to convey everything we need to know about them. Look back at the conversation on page 43 and consider how – with relatively little change – this could be turned into a script. You might want to change things like, "exploded Francis" to (*explosively*) as a stage direction next to Francis's name in the margin, but probably not much else.

How to do it ...

A script, whether a play or an interview, needs to do two things. It needs a) to convey information and b) to convey the personalities of the people speaking. An interviewer should normally be discreet, i.e. not reveal much about themselves. The point of an interview is to draw information out of the interviewee, not to display the great personality of the interviewer!

Playscripts

Here is a short extract from a children's play. Read it through and see how much you can tell about the characters from the way it is written:

Court Duster:	It's the Chief Gardener, your Majestic Sereneness. He'd like a word with you.
King Dingle:	Oh, not now, Duster! I'm just going to have my porridge! And then I'm going to play Dragons with the Prime Minister.
Court Duster:	He seems very bothered, your Magnificence. And he's dropping mud everywhere.
King Dingle:	Oh dratfungus! Let him in then but he mustn't shout at me!
Court Duster:	The Gardener, your Overwhelmingness.
King Dingle:	What is it, Gardener? This is most inconvenient.
Chief Gardener:	(*holding up two huge carrots with bites out of them*) I'm very sorry, your Importantness but this won't wait. Just tell me, just you tell me what you're going to do about this! It's not that I haven't told you before. I've told you and told you. But now it's gone too far. These Monster Rabbits will stop at nothing!

"*Inventing really evil people is great fun.*"

Mary Wesley

Exercises

Now practise!

Here are some exercises you can try to help practise your own skills in scripting.

1 Open any novel of your choice and find a part which has a long passage of conversation of at least 2 pages and, if possible, between at least 3 people. Turn this into a passage of scripted dialogue – like a play. You may need to alter some of the dialogue and to add directions to help the actors.

2 Look back at pages 44–45 on persuasion. Write one or more of the following as play scenes:

a) The teachers at Grimley High School try to persuade the Head to let them organise a fireworks evening.

b) Dan tries to persuade his parents to let him go on a camping weekend with John and Ijah.

c) Mr Robinski tries to persuade Mrs Chinwicket to go out on a date.

d) Mr Sly Red-Fox tries to persuade Mrs Dimsie Chicken to come to dinner.

e) A burglar Deepak, Neelam and John have caught tries to persuade them to let him go.

Remember to set these out in script form!

2

TEXT – WRITING | Scripting

In Sections 2 and 3 we looked at play scenes and scripting. The same technique of putting a name in the left-hand margin and the text in the main part of the page can be used for interviews.

Interviews

An interviewer needs to have his or her questions prepared before the interview begins. This means that some careful research may need to be done on the interviewee's background or circumstances before the meeting. A good interviewer will also be flexible enough to ask unprepared questions if something interesting is said by the interviewee about which they want to find out more.

Look at as many newspapers and magazines as possible and see how they present interviews. A really interesting and revealing interview needs skilful preparation and presentation. Finally, an interview only really works if the interviewer is genuinely interested in the interviewee.

"Interviews are an art form in themselves."

Margaret Atwood

Exercises

Now practise!

3 Ideally, you will be able to do some real-life interviews. *Anyone* can be interviewed – parents, grandparents, neighbours, teachers, friends – as everyone has a story to tell. If you know someone who has done something really unusual, that is even better! Ask nicely and see if they'll let you ask them some questions. Grandparents are often the best bet and you'll discover all kinds of things about your grandparents and their earlier lives you'd never have guessed!

Think carefully about your interviewee before you meet them. Prepare an orderly list of maybe 10 or 12 questions. They should not be the kind of questions that will get a "yes" or "no" answer – that will not result in an interesting interview! So don't ask, "were you born in Russia?" but do ask, "I understand you were born in Russia. What are your earliest memories of that country?" Get it? Try to ask a mixture of questions concerning facts/thoughts/opinions/feelings/other memories, etc. so that your interview has depth and variety. You may want to tape or video your interview or to write notes as you go along.

Either way, present it as far as you can as a professional interview, keeping the interviewer as discreet as possible and allowing the interviewee to come across as realistically as possible.

1

4 You can also make up interviews. This can be fun and really allows your imagination to go wild! Who – in your wildest dreams – would you like to interview? Who would be a nightmare to interview? You may like to write interviews with characters from books or films. Just imagine ...

1

4
TOTAL

55

TEXT – WRITING | Recounting experience

If someone tells you about their holiday, it can be deadly boring or really interesting and entertaining. If you receive a photocopied Christmas letter, it could be a dull list of what they've done and where they've been or full of character, wit and real interest. What makes the difference? This is a difficult question to answer, but one way of trying to answer it is to think about what *you* would find interesting and enjoyable to read. How much detail – and of what kind – would *you* want to read?

How to do it ...

Think about your own memorable experiences. Was it actually what *happened* that made it so special or was it the feelings you had, the anticipation beforehand, the excitement, surprise, etc. and maybe even *how* it happened? These are important questions for anyone who writes factual accounts, most obviously for journalists who need to capture the look and feel of a scene rather than just giving facts and statistics.

Suppose you were asked to give an account of your day at a zoo, theme park, farm, holiday resort or some such place. You could just list all the rides you went on, animals you saw, games you played and so on. Or you could try to help your reader to "see" the place or to "feel" what you felt when you were there. Describing what you see and explaining what you feel are great ways of involving a reader with what you write.

Here are two short passages giving accounts of the same event. The first recounts, literally, what happened. It's pretty uninteresting, I think you'll agree. The second includes detail of what was seen and felt. Any experience can be made to seem dull – or the opposite – depending on how it is written about.

Because I hurt my neck when I fell off the trampoline, we had to go to the doctor. First we queued at reception, then we sat down and waited. After about twenty minutes my name went up and we went to see the doctor. She felt my neck and made me move it about as much as I could. She told me to take painkillers and said I should see a physiotherapist. I didn't go back to school and we went home.

My neck was so painful as I lay on the floor, I couldn't get up on my own. Mum had to leave work and came to collect me. We had to go to the doctor's as an emergency, which was scary, and I was terrified they'd send me to the hospital. Last time we spent nine hours in casualty over my brother's toe! The car was agony. I felt every stone we drove over. In the waiting room I almost forgot the pain. The man next to me had an appalling cough. Each cough lasted about a minute and was like a concert, incredibly loud and full of weird, wheezy and exploding noises. I probably caught something awful! There was a toddler who kept banging his toy in my lap. His mum didn't seem to notice and mine was getting really steamed up. Finally, we were called and a nice, gentle doctor with amazing eyebrows felt my neck and made me try to move it. I think at one point I screamed! She gave me painkillers and an appointment with a physio. It was quite a relief to be told to stay off school for a few days.

"Comment is free but facts are sacred."

C.P. Scott

Exercises

Now practise!

Accounts of experience can, of course, be real or imaginary. The same techniques, though, are needed in each case. It's probably *harder* to write about something that really happened, as you need to remember accurately to be able to select the bits that will make it come alive for a reader. Imaginary accounts are easier in that you invent everything! This page is concerned with your accounts of real experience and gives some ideas for practice. Remember that *everything* can be made interesting if you approach it in the right way.

1 Write a page about your feet. Describe them as though you were a Glumbat from Planet Krampok who had never seen human feet before.

2 Write a page about the face of an older person. Ask a grandparent or, perhaps, someone over sixty if you can study their face carefully and write about it in detail. You can also do this by observing a good photograph.

3 Describe your room as though you are a spider looking at it from a top corner. Think about how this would change the view.

4 Write a page about what you have done in the last hour. Even if it was just watching TV or eating a meal, try to recall every detail – how you sat, who said what, how you felt, who annoyed you, who pleased you or interrupted you, etc.

4

5 A Day in the Life of My Shoes

6 Dinner with My Family

7 The Last Time I Went Shopping

8 The Worst/Best Day of My Holiday

9 The Worst Day of My Life

10 Write a page for each of the following and remember to think DETAIL!
Washing the Car, Mowing the Lawn, Going to the Tip, Pumping up my Tyres

11 Think of something that you have done that involved at least two other people. It could be something like a visit to the doctor or dentist, a day out or a visit to friends. Then write about the occasion from three different points of view, for example yours, the dentist's and your parent's.

12 Imagine you are a burglar exploring your home. Describe the burglar's experience, i.e. see your home from someone else's point of view!

8

12
TOTAL

TEXT – WRITING | Letters – formal and informal

Letter writing is an essential skill. Whether or not you live in the sort of family in which "thank you" letters are written, you will know that everyone, at some time or other, has to – or wants to – write letters. And, of course, plenty of them come through your letter box!

How to do it ...

It's important to know the appropriate style of writing, i.e. the words you use, the grammar and the tone, for different types of letters. For example, if you were dropping a note to a friend to remind them to bring warm clothes for a birthday outing you would use a different tone and language than if you were writing to your Head Teacher to apologise for smashing a window. Similarly, if you attended Grimley High School and you wanted to write a letter to the local MP about it being closed down, you would choose yet a different tone and style.

The point is that the language you use needs to be appropriate for the type of letter you are writing and what you want it to achieve. It's like clothes. You wouldn't wear your coolest clothes and new trainers for carrying garden rubbish to the council dump, would you? Here are two examples of letters written in the wrong language:

Hi!

Mr Snapperchild says I've got to say sorry for smashing the window but it wasn't my fault. Dan did it. I just got in the way and the ball bounced off me so why do I have to say sorry? You better not say I've got to pay for it cos my dad'll go mad. It had a crack in it anyway so what's the big deal? Anyway, why can't we have crisps in break any more?

Yours faithfully,

Andy

9 Grimley Road,
Grimley,
GR3 7YH

Mrs F. Doddery,
Pinkerton Avenue,
Trembly,
TR7 9YH

14th March

Dear Grandmother,

As you know I am coming to see you next weekend. I am writing to let you know that I will be arriving by train on Saturday March 17th at 11.40 a.m. and it would be most convenient if you could collect me. I am looking forward to seeing you and Granddad as it seems a long time since Christmas. Thank you for the video. I have watched it six times as it is very good.

Yours sincerely,
Andrew

The first letter, to the Head Teacher, should be set out properly, whereas the second letter, to Andy's granny, need not be so formal. Rewrite both these letters in a format and a style more appropriate to the jobs they have to do.

"More than kisses, letters mingle souls."
John Donne

Exercises

Now practise!

Formal letters need to be set out formally, i.e. with your address in the top right-hand corner, the name and address of the person you are writing to just below on the left-hand side and the date opposite the *Dear Sir* or *Dear Mrs Smith* or other greeting. The letter needs proper paragraphing and to be clear and precise. Letters to friends and family don't need this formality. The important thing is to know *how* to write each type of letter appropriately.

1   Write a properly laid-out formal letter to the Member of Parliament for Grimley asking for her support in either a) getting Grimley High School closed down or b) helping to keep it open. Plan your argument before you start writing to ensure it's well thought out and sounds sensible and persuasive.

2   Imagine Prince Charles has taken you on a tour of Buckingham Palace. Perhaps there was a banquet thrown in too! Write a letter thanking him for the whole occasion. (You may need to invent some details of the tour if you're not familiar with the inside of Buckingham Palace!)

3   You recently bought a box of toffee bars to put in party bags but, when you opened the box, the bars were all squashed. Write a letter of complaint to the manager of the supermarket.

4   The local football club has withdrawn its cheap seats for under 16s. You are a keen fan. Write a letter to the manager of the club asking him to reconsider.

5   You missed a school lesson last week because you found an injured cat and you took it to the vet. Write a letter to your very cross teacher to apologise and explain what happened.

5

Exercises

Now practise!

6 You have been allocated a new pen pal in Hungary. Write your first letter – remember his English is not as good or as colloquial as yours – in which you give lots of detail about yourself and your life, and also you ask him about himself.

7 Write a letter to your hero or heroine.

8 Your favourite cousin is moving 300 miles to live near you. She will probably come to your school. Write to tell her about your town and about how you feel about it. Think about the sorts of things you would want to know if you were her.

9 One of your parents is working abroad for six months. Write a letter to tell him or her your news. Do you miss him or her?

10 Your aunt and uncle have sent you an unbelievably wonderful present – exactly what you've always wanted. Write and thank them.

5

10
TOTAL

61

TEXT – WRITING | Fiction I

The bones

You will have been told many times that stories need a beginning, a middle and an end. True, of course. But where to begin? What happens in the middle? Where to end? If you don't see yourself as a naturally brilliant story writer, these may seem hard questions to answer. The next four pages will help you to plan stories and then to write a story.

How to do it ...

Think of a story as a skeleton. The backbone – the main idea – is what holds the whole thing together. But the story also needs feet and legs, a pelvis, a rib cage, arms, shoulders, a collarbone and a head. (Better not bother too much about all the smaller bones!) A short story, like the ones you might write, i.e. shorter than a whole novel, needs a simple structure – not too many bones! It will, however, need a strong, straight backbone, that is, a strong, clear main idea. What actually *happens* in your story is the structure – the plot. This is what you can plan, simply, before you start to write. You can use a diagram or a list – whatever suits you best. Look at the example below.

Mr Snapperchild's Holiday

Mr S books a holiday at Grimley Tours

Arrives at airport – long delay

Check-in assistant goes to find out why

Pilot is cowering under desk – he is ex-pupil of Mr S – has seen his name on passenger list

Substitute pilot found

Mr S settles into seat – no idea what has been going on

Here are some other ideas that may help:

1 Unless you are writing a full-length novel it is not helpful to give masses of information about your main character at the start. If the information is necessary it can evolve during the course of the story. But – is it really necessary? Is it part of your story's main idea?

2 It's not always necessary to start telling the story at its actual beginning. You can start the writing right in the middle of an exciting part, for example "I ran after him as fast as I could, but he'd vanished ..." and then fill in what has led up to this moment afterwards in a kind of flashback technique. This grabs the attention of your reader right at the start.

3 Consider whether your story might be best told in the first or the third person. It can make a big difference to how you present your characters, especially if there are more than one or two.

4 All stories include some kind of *conflict*, maybe between individuals or maybe inside someone – perhaps they have to make a decision? At what point in your story do you want this conflict resolved? Often it's somewhere between the middle and the end, but some stories leave it right to the last minute.

"When I want to read a novel, I write one."

Benjamin Disraeli

Exercises

Now practise!

1   Look back at the plan on page 62. Then write similar plans for the following stories. Yours should include between 4 and 7 points. Try to keep your story in one place and to one or two action scenes. This is to avoid "... back home ... later that day ... in the Australian outback ... three weeks later ...", etc. And remember to keep to one main idea!

   a) *The Magic Boots*

   b) *My Try Out with Manchester United (or another team if you're fussy!)*

   c) *Lost on the Underground*

   d) *Going Fishing*

   e) *Deepak's Dog*

   f) *A Morning in Accident and Emergency*

   g) *Mrs Chinwicket's Birthday*

   h) *The Day the Camel Escaped from the Zoo*

`8`

2   Think about each one of your plans in turn. At which point could the actual telling of the story start? For example, the story planned out on page 66 could actually start, "Mr Snapperchild settled comfortably into his seat. The delay had ruffled him a bit but everything seemed fine now. He decided not to concern himself with whatever the problem had been." Or the story could begin at the point when the first pilot reads Mr Snapperchild's name on the list. Do you see? So – think through all your plans and work out where it might be most fun to start your stories.

3   Think about first and third person narratives. Which would you use with each story?

4   Look carefully again at your plans. How long do you feel each story would be? Sometimes you'll be asked to write a certain number of words or pages or you'll have a time limit. It's important to have an idea of how much time you'd need for any individual story. Sometimes a writer may run out of ideas after only half a page or find that the story is going to be book-length! Can you assess how long each of your stories will need to be? This is the time to cross out plans which you feel you could not develop into stories of between 3 and 6 pages of writing.

5   Now choose the plan you like best and write it out as a full story. Limit your writing to between 3 and 6 pages.

6   Consider your ending. Does the story end at the right time? In the right place? What kind of end did you aim for – mysterious, funny, horrible? Then think about when and how you would want to end the stories in your list of plans.

`5`

`13`
`TOTAL`

TEXT – WRITING | Fiction II

The flesh!

Right! So you've got your idea, you've got your plan, you know what's going to happen and you know – more or less – how and when it will end. Some people find this the easy part but find it much harder to write a story that's more than just a list of what happens, as in the example below:

> *Ijah woke up. He went to school. In break he played football. A man was watching and talking to the Head Teacher. After break the Head called Ijah over and the man asked him if he'd like a trial with Grimley Town FC Juniors Squad. Ijah said yes but he'd have to ask his mum ... etc.*

How to do it ...

The story above seems to have a structure, one good main idea and so on but, as a piece of writing, it's flat and dull. In other words, the bones are OK but bare. This story needs flesh! So how to beef it up? For this story, you might like to think about the following.

a) What kind of day was it?

b) How did Ijah feel when he went to school?

c) Did he notice the Head and the man in break?

d) What might he have noticed about them if he did spot them?

e) How was the football going?

f) What actually happened when the Head called him over?

Exercises

Now practise!

1   Look back again at the plans you made on page 63. Taking each one in turn, think about the following.

a) **The setting**. Does this story need a background of some kind? Where does it happen? Somewhere familiar? Somewhere exotic? Might a reader need help in "picturing" the place? It may be clear in *your* mind but that doesn't mean a reader will "see" it, without your help! Even a few words can make the difference, for example "The tall trees swayed under the tropical sun", or, "the prison cell was damp and cold".

b) **The weather**. Weather is great for helping to create a particular mood and atmosphere. A story about a birthday outing, for example, will begin very differently if it starts with "The wind blasted furiously around the house ..." than if it starts with "The sun gently warmed the garden ..."!

c) **Your senses**. Remember you can smell, see, hear, feel and taste – and so can your characters! Think about breakfast cereals – as many as you can. Think how differently they look, smell, feel, taste and *sound*! What words for these sensations can you find? Try to use that awareness in the way you write about your characters' experiences.

d) **Your characters**. What do they look like? How do they dress? How do they move? How do they talk? Your reader will need a little help in "seeing" them – you will need to give a few details. What about their personalities? Are they nervy, calm, lively, friendly, grumpy? What words can you use in each case?

4

TEXT – WRITING | Fiction II

Let's try the story from page 64 again.

"C'mon girl! C'mon girl! C'mon gir-ir-irlll! Da Da Da-da-da-Dah!" Ijah's radio snapped on at the loudest section of a song he didn't like. He shook his head, blinked and realised it must be getting-up-time. He crawled out of bed, hauled on his clothes and nipped into the bathroom before anyone else got in. The rain was battering the window. Ijah slithered down the stairs and munched through two large bowlfuls of cereal.

"Hurry up!" shouted Sonia. "We're leaving in ONE minute." Ijah pulled on his jacket and dashed, head down, to the car.

By the time break came, he'd woken up properly and the rain had stopped. Maths had been quite good and History had been very good but now was The Final – 6T against 6S – and he was the leading 6T striker.

John blew the whistle and Ijah took the first kick. It was going really well and he made a brilliant long pass to Deepak who shot just past the post. The second chance was better and Dan just tapped the ball past the 6S goalie. Break ended too soon, though, and the second half would have to wait till lunch. Ijah was just heading for the door to the cloakrooms when he noticed the Head was waving him over. His heart sank – was he wearing the wrong shoes? She had a man in a super-cool track suit with her. He was a little on the overweight side and heavy on the stubble but, somehow, impressive.

"Ijah," said the Head, "this is Mr Vernon from Grimley Town Football Club. He wants to talk to you ..."

"Fiction is nothing less than the subtlest instrument for self-examination and self-display that mankind has invented yet."

John Updike

Exercises

Now practise!

1 Here are two more important points about writing fiction to consider.

a) Sometimes it's helpful and interesting to see the characters from the point of view of other characters. You can show different sides of them or of a situation if you show how different people are affected by what is happening.

b) Conversation is useful, as we have seen on pages 42 and 43, in breaking up story-telling and in allowing characters to reveal their personalities and relationships. The characters can also talk *about* each other. You will need some good conversation in your stories. For example, in the story about Ijah on page 66, we *could* have had:

"Is that him, there?" asked Joe Vernon. "The kid in the yellow rugby shirt?"
"That's Ijah, yes," said the Head, a little proudly.
"He's got rubber legs, he has."
"He's a very modest boy, too."
"You'd think that ball was glued to his boots. And he's fast! Let's have him over ..."

All these are ways of putting flesh on your story plans. Now, go through your plans on page 63 and try to write out each one as a full story. Don't overdo the detail. You need just enough to help the reader imagine your characters and their settings for themselves. You should now be able to write well-planned, lively stories. Good luck! Happy writing!

8

TEXT – WRITING | **Section practice**

1   Re-read a book you liked when you were younger – maybe a year or more ago. Write a review of it which would help a younger child decide whether he or she wanted to read it. (Remind yourself of the guidelines on pages 50–51 first.)

2   "One can never read the same book twice," goes an old saying. This has a meaning beyond the obvious surface one. What does it mean to you? Write a page or so giving your thoughts and experiences.

3   Write a script for three or more voices on one or more of the following subjects:

      a)   In the Staffroom

      b)   Planning a Holiday

      c)   The Fight

      d)   An Afternoon on Planet Krampok

4   Invent an interview between yourself and one or more of the following:

      a)   A Famous Person from History

      b)   A Sports or Show Business Personality or other well-known person in whom you are interested

      c)   Yourself at the age of 50 and a younger interviewer

      d)   After some careful research into:

          i)   a famous explorer or

         ii)   a famous inventor or

        iii)   a famous scientist

      construct an interview with them.

4

TEXT – WRITING | Section practice

5 a) A Day in the Life of Me

   Tell the story of your typical day in such a way as to make it lively and interesting. Think of people, places, incidents, conversations and so on.

   b) A Day in the Life of My Hand (choose your left or right, as you please)

6 a) A present you ordered for your sister's birthday did not arrive in time, much to her disappointment and your annoyance. Write a letter to the company giving details of what you ordered and when, explaining the effects of their inefficiency.

   b) Your teacher coached you individually for a special exam or audition or trial which went very well. Write a letter thanking them and telling them how it went.

7 Write plans for the following titles. Remember to keep to one main idea and to have between 4 and 6 points in each plan. Imagine essays that would take 30–40 minutes to write in full.

   a) Moving House   b) The Day I Spent as a Rat

   c) The Magic Telephone   d) The Haircut

   e) The Flood

8 Now write two of the plans from Exercise 7 as full stories. Choose one to write in the first person and one to write in the third person.

10

14
TOTAL

TEST | Paper One

The questions on this paper should be answered on this and the following page.

1. Here is a passage in which there are many spelling mistakes. There is also no punctuation. Correct it carefully. You will need to correct 25 spellings. There are more than 80 corrections to punctuation, including writing *NL* for *New Line* where appropriate and adding capital letters. You can use the space at the bottom of the page to try out spellings.

there had been no snow for years most of the children had never seen it befor so they couldnt concerntrate in lessens once it began Ijah mist the beggining and at first he wasnt shure what it was finaly the teacher let them go outside however she said very firmly no snow down peoples necks everyone I dont want any acsidents Ijah found Dan its such a suprise he said we didnt ever have snow in jamaica Dan agreed its pretty unusal and its beautifull they met Neelam who looked teriffied its dangerouse she complained its extremley slippery and horible and you cant walk propaly dan picked up some snow and put it on his tonge mmm delishus he said look over there who is it where asked Neelam oh its john dont you reconise him john had got a hat puled down over his eyes Id be embarased to go out like that said Ijah your just jelous said dan come on he descided its time to make a moutain

100

2 Your new pen-pal is a Glumbat from Planet Krampok. He is intelligent and understands a lot about Earth life but every now and again he needs an explanation of something you have mentioned. In no more than three or four sentences each, try to explain: a) a chair, b) a carpet, c) a door, d) a post box, e) an egg, f) a dream, g) snow.

28

TEST | Paper Two

Read the passage and answer the questions on this and the following page. You may use extra paper if you need to.

It's remarkable how a mountain, and not, after all, a very large one, which can look gentle and inviting on bright, warm days, can be so menacing and even dangerous when the weather is bad. I had taken many visitors to the top of Crackdown over the years and we had looked out over the hilltops to the ribbon of silver which is the Irish Sea, about twenty miles off to the West. So when Mike and Jane set off that morning, I wasn't worried. It was bright and clear. They knew the common sense things – proper boots, a good map, keeping an eye out for weather changes and so on. I said I'd stay in, partly to give them some time on their own – city life doesn't provide much of that – partly to prepare the good vegetable soup I rather pride myself on and partly to finish an article I was writing. So I wasn't, despite twenty years of living here, expecting the sudden darkening of the skies, the hurling of hailstones against the house and the virtual disappearance of Crackdown in a blanket of mist.

I'd expected them back for lunch, but at two I ate my soup alone. From then on it was just waiting. When the phone rang at half past four I jumped at it.

"It's me, Jane," said a remote-sounding voice, higher and somehow smaller than usual. "We're in Pengarth," (a small town about eight miles away) "we've just arrived – by ambulance."

"Good God!"

"We're OK but....it's been quite a day......."

a) Explain in your own words the comparison the writer makes in the long first sentence: --
----

`1`

b) What could be seen from the top of Crackdown? --------------------------------
----

`1`

c) Why wasn't the writer worried when his visitors set off for their walk? ....

--- **1**

d) Give, briefly, his three reasons for not going with them: ---------------------------------

----

--- **3**

e) Do you think that the writer should have been prepared for the weather to change?

--- **1**

f) What do you think the writer's feelings were from the time the rain started and the phone call? --

----

--- **1**

g) Find three prepositional phrases in the passage: ---------------------------------------

----

--- **3**

h) Find:

i) a sentence composed of just one main clause ---------------------------------------

----

ii) a subordinate adverbial clause of time ---

----

iii) a sentence composed of two main clauses ---

--- **3**

i) Continue the conversation from the end of the passage on a separate sheet of paper.

1

15
TOTAL

TEST | Paper Three

1   Choose one of the following titles and write a plan of between 4 and 6 points. (You may need to look ahead at question 2 to help in your choice of question.)

   a) The New Machine

   b) The Competition

   c) Building the Shed

   d) Back in Time

   e) Neighbours

6

2   Now write out your plan as a full story in the **first person**. You may choose to write it as a series of diary extracts or of letters, or just as a straightforward narrative. You may use extra paper if necessary.

10

3 Now write a newspaper report (i.e. in the third person) giving an account of part or the whole of your story. You may use extra paper if you need it.

10

26
TOTAL